SAP Business One
Complete Self-Assessment Guide

G000094324

The guidance in this Self-Assessment is base
practices and standards in business process architecture, design and
quality management. The guidance is also based on the professional
judgment of the individual collaborators listed in the Acknowledgments.

Notice of rights

Trademarks

Table of Contents

About The Art of Service

The Art of Service, Business Process Architects since 2000, is dedicated to helping stakeholders achieve excellence.

Defining, designing, creating, and implementing a process to solve a stakeholders challenge or meet an objective is the most valuable role… In EVERY group, company, organization and department.

Unless you're talking a one-time, single-use project, there should be a process. Whether that process is managed and implemented by humans, AI, or a combination of the two, it needs to be designed by someone with a complex enough perspective to ask the right questions.

Someone capable of asking the right questions and step back and say, 'What are we really trying to accomplish here? And is there a different way to look at it?'

With The Art of Service's Standard Requirements Self-Assessments, we empower people who can do just that — whether their title is marketer, entrepreneur, manager, salesperson, consultant, Business Process Manager, executive assistant, IT Manager, CIO etc... —they are the people who rule the future. They are people who watch the process as it happens, and ask the right questions to make the process work better.

Contact us when you need any support with this Self-Assessment and any help with templates, blue-prints and examples of standard documents you might need:

http://theartofservice.com
service@theartofservice.com

Acknowledgments

This checklist was developed under the auspices of The Art of Service, chaired by Gerardus Blokdyk.

Representatives from several client companies participated in the preparation of this Self-Assessment.

In addition, we are thankful for the design and printing services provided.

Included Resources - how to access

Included with your purchase of the book is the SAP Business One Self-Assessment Spreadsheet Dashboard which contains all questions and Self-Assessment areas and auto-generates insights, graphs, and project RACI planning - all with examples to get you started right away.

How? Simply send an email to
access@theartofservice.com
with this books' title in the subject to get the SAP Business One Self Assessment Tool right away.

You will receive the following contents with New and Updated specific criteria:

• The latest quick edition of the book in PDF

• The latest complete edition of the book in PDF, which criteria correspond to the criteria in...

• The Self-Assessment Excel Dashboard, and...

• Example pre-filled Self-Assessment Excel Dashboard to get familiar with results generation

• In-depth specific Checklists covering the topic

• Project management checklists and templates to assist with implementation

INCLUDES LIFETIME SELF ASSESSMENT UPDATES

Every self assessment comes with Lifetime Updates and Lifetime Free Updated Books. Lifetime Updates is an industry-first feature which allows you to receive verified self assessment updates, ensuring you always have the most accurate information at your fingertips.

Get it now- you will be glad you did - do it now, before you forget.

Send an email to **access@theartofservice.com** with this books' title in the subject to get the SAP Business One Self Assessment Tool right away.

Your feedback is invaluable to us

If you recently bought this book, we would love to hear from you! You can do this by writing a review on amazon (or the online store where you purchased this book) about your last purchase! As part of our continual service improvement process, we love to hear real client experiences and feedback.

How does it work?
To post a review on Amazon, just log in to your account and click on the Create Your Own Review button (under Customer Reviews) of the relevant product page. You can find examples of product reviews in Amazon. If you purchased from another online store, simply follow their procedures.

What happens when I submit my review?
Once you have submitted your review, send us an email at review@theartofservice.com with the link to your review so we can properly thank you for your feedback.

Purpose of this Self-Assessment

This Self-Assessment has been developed to improve understanding of the requirements and elements of SAP Business One, based on best practices and standards in business process architecture, design and quality management.

It is designed to allow for a rapid Self-Assessment to determine how closely existing management practices and procedures correspond to the elements of the Self-Assessment.

The criteria of requirements and elements of SAP Business One have been rephrased in the format of a Self-Assessment questionnaire, with a seven-criterion scoring system, as explained in this document.

In this format, even with limited background knowledge of SAP

Business One, a manager can quickly review existing operations to determine how they measure up to the standards. This in turn can serve as the starting point of a 'gap analysis' to identify management tools or system elements that might usefully be implemented in the organization to help improve overall performance.

How to use the Self-Assessment

On the following pages are a series of questions to identify to what extent your SAP Business One initiative is complete in comparison to the requirements set in standards.

To facilitate answering the questions, there is a space in front of each question to enter a score on a scale of '1' to '5'.

1 Strongly Disagree

2 Disagree

3 Neutral

4 Agree

5 Strongly Agree

Read the question and rate it with the following in front of mind:

'In my belief,
the answer to this question is clearly defined'.

There are two ways in which you can choose to interpret this statement;
1. how aware are you that the answer to the question is clearly defined
2. for more in-depth analysis you can choose to gather

evidence and confirm the answer to the question. This obviously will take more time, most Self-Assessment users opt for the first way to interpret the question and dig deeper later on based on the outcome of the overall Self-Assessment.

A score of '1' would mean that the answer is not clear at all, where a '5' would mean the answer is crystal clear and defined. Leave emtpy when the question is not applicable or you don't want to answer it, you can skip it without affecting your score. Write your score in the space provided.

After you have responded to all the appropriate statements in each section, compute your average score for that section, using the formula provided, and round to the nearest tenth. Then transfer to the corresponding spoke in the SAP Business One Scorecard on the second next page of the Self-Assessment.

Your completed SAP Business One Scorecard will give you a clear presentation of which SAP Business One areas need attention.

SAP Business One
Scorecard Example

Example of how the finalized Scorecard can look like:

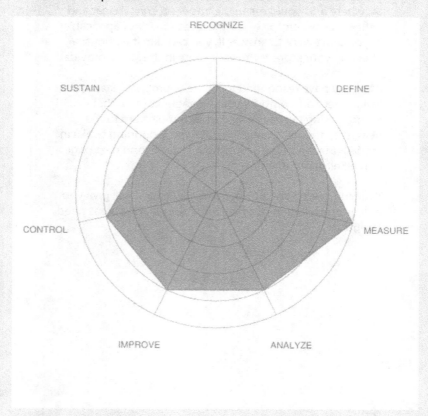

SAP Business One
Scorecard

Your Scores:

BEGINNING OF THE SELF-ASSESSMENT:

CRITERION #1: RECOGNIZE

INTENT: Be aware of the need for change. Recognize that there is an unfavorable variation, problem or symptom.

In my belief, the answer to this question is clearly defined:

5 Strongly Agree

4 Agree

3 Neutral

2 Disagree

1 Strongly Disagree

1. Have you identified your SAP Business One key performance indicators?
<--- Score

2. Structure: How large & dispersed, how tightly integrated does it need to be?
<--- Score

3. How do we Identify specific SAP Business One

investment and emerging trends?
<--- Score

4. What should be considered when identifying available resources, constraints, and deadlines?
<--- Score

5. How are the SAP Business One's objectives aligned to the group's overall stakeholder strategy?
<--- Score

6. How will your ERP platform deliver the information needed?
<--- Score

7. How are we going to measure success?
<--- Score

8. Are there any specific expectations or concerns about the SAP Business One team, SAP Business One itself?
<--- Score

9. What else needs to be measured?
<--- Score

10. Does our organization need more SAP Business One education?
<--- Score

11. Are controls defined to recognize and contain problems?
<--- Score

12. What are the stakeholder objectives to be achieved with SAP Business One?

<--- Score

13. What do we need to start doing?
<--- Score

14. What would happen if SAP Business One weren't done?
<--- Score

15. How do I know I need an erp system?
<--- Score

16. How do you assess your SAP Business One workforce capability and capacity needs, including skills, competencies, and staffing levels?
<--- Score

17. Who defines the rules in relation to any given issue?
<--- Score

18. Can Management personnel recognize the monetary benefit of SAP Business One?
<--- Score

19. Why do we need to keep records?
<--- Score

20. Will it solve real problems?
<--- Score

21. What vendors make products that address the SAP Business One needs?
<--- Score

22. What management, organization, and

technology issues should be addressed in deciding whether to use a conventional ERP or CRM system versus a cloud-based version?
<--- Score

23. Will a response program recognize when a crisis occurs and provide some level of response?
<--- Score

24. Who needs to know about SAP Business One ?
<--- Score

25. What training and capacity building actions are needed to implement proposed reforms?
<--- Score

26. Who else hopes to benefit from it?
<--- Score

27. Are there recognized SAP Business One problems?
<--- Score

28. For your SAP Business One project, identify and describe the business environment. is there more than one layer to the business environment?
<--- Score

29. How does it fit into our organizational needs and tasks?
<--- Score

30. What tools and technologies are needed for a custom SAP Business One project?
<--- Score

31. Will new equipment/products be required to

facilitate SAP Business One delivery for example is new software needed?

<--- Score

32. What problems are you facing and how do you consider SAP Business One will circumvent those obstacles?

<--- Score

33. When a SAP Business One manager recognizes a problem, what options are available?

<--- Score

34. Are there SAP Business One problems defined?

<--- Score

35. What are the main benefits (and dis-benefits) that you have identified to date?

<--- Score

36. How much are sponsors, customers, partners, stakeholders involved in SAP Business One? In other words, what are the risks, if SAP Business One does not deliver successfully?

<--- Score

37. Will SAP Business One deliverables need to be tested and, if so, by whom?

<--- Score

38. Find a story of problems encountered with an ERP implementation. What factors contributed to the obstacles which were encountered?

<--- Score

39. Cloud management for SAP Business One do

we really need one?
<--- Score

40. What are the expected benefits of SAP Business One to the stakeholder?
<--- Score

41. Consider your own SAP Business One project. what types of organizational problems do you think might be causing or affecting your problem, based on the work done so far?
<--- Score

42. As a sponsor, customer or management, how important is it to meet goals, objectives?
<--- Score

43. What does SAP Business One success mean to the stakeholders?
<--- Score

44. What are the main problems or barriers that are delaying progress with your project/ implementation?
<--- Score

45. What situation(s) led to this SAP Business One Self Assessment?
<--- Score

46. How do you identify the kinds of information that you will need?
<--- Score

47. How can auditing be a preventative security measure?

<--- Score

48. What prevents me from making the changes I know will make me a more effective SAP Business One leader?
<--- Score

49. What is the smallest subset of the problem we can usefully solve?
<--- Score

50. How do you identify the information basis for later specification of performance or acceptance criteria?
<--- Score

51. Does SAP Business One create potential expectations in other areas that need to be recognized and considered?
<--- Score

52. Think about the people you identified for your SAP Business One project and the project responsibilities you would assign to them. what kind of training do you think they would need to perform these responsibilities effectively?
<--- Score

53. What information do users need?
<--- Score

54. What Problem Does an ERP System Solve?
<--- Score

55. Is it clear when you think of the day ahead of you what activities and tasks you need to

complete?
<--- Score

56. Do we know what we need to know about this topic?
<--- Score

57. How soon do you need things to stabilise fully after going live in an ERP implementation?
<--- Score

Add up total points for this section:
_____ = Total points for this section

Divided by: _____ (number of statements answered) = _____
Average score for this section

Transfer your score to the SAP Business One Index at the beginning of the Self-Assessment.

CRITERION #2: DEFINE:

INTENT: Formulate the stakeholder problem. Define the problem, needs and objectives.

In my belief, the answer to this question is clearly defined:

5 Strongly Agree

4 Agree

3 Neutral

2 Disagree

1 Strongly Disagree

1. Has the SAP Business One work been fairly and/or equitably divided and delegated among team members who are qualified and capable to perform the work? Has everyone contributed?
<--- Score

2. Is data collected and displayed to better understand customer(s) critical needs and requirements.
<--- Score

3. Will team members regularly document their SAP Business One work?
<--- Score

4. How feasible is cloud erp and where can one find some noteworthy deployment examples?
<--- Score

5. Are roles and responsibilities formally defined?
<--- Score

6. Are different versions of process maps needed to account for the different types of inputs?
<--- Score

7. Is the improvement team aware of the different versions of a process: what they think it is vs. what it actually is vs. what it should be vs. what it could be?
<--- Score

8. When are meeting minutes sent out? Who is on the distribution list?
<--- Score

9. Are team charters developed?
<--- Score

10. When is the estimated completion date?
<--- Score

11. Are customer(s) identified and segmented according to their different needs and requirements?
<--- Score

12. Is the team sponsored by a champion or

stakeholder leader?
<--- Score

13. Has a high-level 'as is' process map been completed, verified and validated?
<--- Score

14. Is the SAP Business One scope manageable?
<--- Score

15. Is there a SAP Business One management charter, including stakeholder case, problem and goal statements, scope, milestones, roles and responsibilities, communication plan?
<--- Score

16. What are the dynamics of the communication plan?
<--- Score

17. Who are the SAP Business One improvement team members, including Management Leads and Coaches?
<--- Score

18. How often are the team meetings?
<--- Score

19. In what way can we redefine the criteria of choice clients have in our category in our favor?
<--- Score

20. Is there a critical path to deliver SAP Business One results?
<--- Score

21. Does the predefined ERP implementation methodology work for us?
<--- Score

22. What customer feedback methods were used to solicit their input?
<--- Score

23. How was the 'as is' process map developed, reviewed, verified and validated?
<--- Score

24. How will variation in the actual durations of each activity be dealt with to ensure that the expected SAP Business One results are met?
<--- Score

25. Are Required Metrics Defined?
<--- Score

26. Is the current 'as is' process being followed? If not, what are the discrepancies?
<--- Score

27. Are customers identified and high impact areas defined?
<--- Score

28. How does the SAP Business One manager ensure against scope creep?
<--- Score

29. Is the team adequately staffed with the desired cross-functionality? If not, what additional resources are available to the team?
<--- Score

30. Are audit criteria, scope, frequency and methods defined?
<--- Score

31. Have all basic functions of SAP Business One been defined?
<--- Score

32. Have specific policy objectives been defined?
<--- Score

33. What baselines are required to be defined and managed?
<--- Score

34. How important is time-to-market for your requirement?
<--- Score

35. Have all of the relationships been defined properly?
<--- Score

36. How would you define the culture here?
<--- Score

37. What critical content must be communicated – who, what, when, where, and how?
<--- Score

38. Has a project plan, Gantt chart, or similar been developed/completed?
<--- Score

39. Are task requirements clearly defined?

<--- Score

40. Has anyone else (internal or external to the group) attempted to solve this problem or a similar one before? If so, what knowledge can be leveraged from these previous efforts?
<--- Score

41. What is scope creep and why is it important to manage during an ERP implementation?
<--- Score

42. Does the team have regular meetings?
<--- Score

43. What constraints exist that might impact the team?
<--- Score

44. How and when will the baselines be defined?
<--- Score

45. Is the scope of SAP Business One defined?
<--- Score

46. Have the customer needs been translated into specific, measurable requirements? How?
<--- Score

47. Is there a completed, verified, and validated high-level 'as is' (not 'should be' or 'could be') stakeholder process map?
<--- Score

48. Are there any constraints known that bear on the ability to perform SAP Business One work? How is the

team addressing them?
<--- Score

49. How did the SAP Business One manager receive input to the development of a SAP Business One improvement plan and the estimated completion dates/times of each activity?
<--- Score

50. What are the Roles and Responsibilities for each team member and its leadership? Where is this documented?
<--- Score

51. Are stakeholder processes mapped?
<--- Score

52. How do you keep key subject matter experts in the loop?
<--- Score

53. Has the improvement team collected the 'voice of the customer' (obtained feedback – qualitative and quantitative)?
<--- Score

54. Are accountability and ownership for SAP Business One clearly defined?
<--- Score

55. What tools and roadmaps did you use for getting through the Define phase?
<--- Score

56. Has a team charter been developed and communicated?

<--- Score

57. Is it clearly defined in and to your organization what you do?
<--- Score

58. What would be the goal or target for a SAP Business One's improvement team?
<--- Score

59. Are there different segments of customers?
<--- Score

60. What are the compelling stakeholder reasons for embarking on SAP Business One?
<--- Score

61. In case multiple ERP systems are in place; could you explain what functions are supported by the ORACLE, PEOPLESOFT and SAP environments, and are their multiple instances of each?
<--- Score

62. How will the SAP Business One team and the group measure complete success of SAP Business One?
<--- Score

63. What are the boundaries of the scope? What is in bounds and what is not? What is the start point? What is the stop point?
<--- Score

64. Are improvement team members fully trained on SAP Business One?
<--- Score

65. Is full participation by members in regularly held team meetings guaranteed?
<--- Score

66. If substitutes have been appointed, have they been briefed on the SAP Business One goals and received regular communications as to the progress to date?
<--- Score

67. When was the SAP Business One start date?
<--- Score

68. Is a fully trained team formed, supported, and committed to work on the SAP Business One improvements?
<--- Score

69. What defines Best in Class?
<--- Score

70. Has/have the customer(s) been identified?
<--- Score

71. How can the value of SAP Business One be defined?
<--- Score

72. Is the team equipped with available and reliable resources?
<--- Score

73. How would one define SAP Business One leadership?
<--- Score

74. In what way can we redefine the criteria of choice in our category in our favor, as Method introduced style and design to cleaning and Virgin America returned glamor to flying?
<--- Score

75. Do we all define SAP Business One in the same way?
<--- Score

76. Is there regularly 100% attendance at the team meetings? If not, have appointed substitutes attended to preserve cross-functionality and full representation?
<--- Score

77. Is SAP Business One Required?
<--- Score

78. Where does scope creep occur and how doe we manage it?
<--- Score

79. Who defines (or who defined) the rules and roles?
<--- Score

80. Are approval levels defined for contracts and supplements to contracts?
<--- Score

81. Is SAP Business One currently on schedule according to the plan?
<--- Score

82. Is the team formed and are team leaders (Coaches

and Management Leads) assigned?
<--- Score

83. What key stakeholder process output measure(s) does SAP Business One leverage and how?
<--- Score

84. What are the rough order estimates on cost savings/opportunities that SAP Business One brings?
<--- Score

85. Is SAP Business One linked to key stakeholder goals and objectives?
<--- Score

86. Will team members perform SAP Business One work when assigned and in a timely fashion?
<--- Score

87. How is the team tracking and documenting its work?
<--- Score

88. What specifically is the problem? Where does it occur? When does it occur? What is its extent?
<--- Score

89. Do the problem and goal statements meet the SMART criteria (specific, measurable, attainable, relevant, and time-bound)?
<--- Score

90. What is the minimum educational requirement for potential new hires?
<--- Score

91. Has the direction changed at all during the course of SAP Business One? If so, when did it change and why?
<--- Score

92. Is there a completed SIPOC representation, describing the Suppliers, Inputs, Process, Outputs, and Customers?
<--- Score

93. Has everyone on the team, including the team leaders, been properly trained?
<--- Score

Add up total points for this section:
_ _ _ _ _ = Total points for this section

Divided by: _ _ _ _ _ _ (number of statements answered) = _ _ _ _ _ _
Average score for this section

Transfer your score to the SAP Business One Index at the beginning of the Self-Assessment.

CRITERION #3: MEASURE:

INTENT: Gather the correct data.
Measure the current performance and
evolution of the situation.

In my belief, the answer to this
question is clearly defined:

5 Strongly Agree

4 Agree

3 Neutral

2 Disagree

1 Strongly Disagree

1. Is data collection planned and executed?
<--- Score

2. Customer Measures: How Do Customers See Us?
<--- Score

**3. What are the uncertainties surrounding
estimates of impact?**
<--- Score

4. Who should receive measurement reports ?
<--- Score

5. Have the types of risks that may impact SAP Business One been identified and analyzed?
<--- Score

6. Will We Aggregate Measures across Priorities?
<--- Score

7. Does SAP Business One analysis isolate the fundamental causes of problems?
<--- Score

8. What will be measured?
<--- Score

9. What is an unallowable cost?
<--- Score

10. How close was the cost of user training and other erp deployment expenses to your original estimate?
<--- Score

11. Meeting the challenge: are missed SAP Business One opportunities costing us money?
<--- Score

12. What are the costs of reform?
<--- Score

13. Can we do SAP Business One without complex (expensive) analysis?
<--- Score

14. Is a solid data collection plan established that includes measurement systems analysis?
<--- Score

15. What is the total cost related to deploying SAP Business One, including any consulting or professional services?
<--- Score

16. Which customers can't participate in our market because they lack skills, wealth, or convenient access to existing solutions?
<--- Score

17. What are my customers expectations and measures?
<--- Score

18. What key measures identified indicate the performance of the stakeholder process?
<--- Score

19. How Will We Measure Success?
<--- Score

20. How will measures be used to manage and adapt?
<--- Score

21. How can we measure the performance?
<--- Score

22. Why should we expend time and effort to implement measurement?
<--- Score

23. Are there any easy-to-implement alternatives to SAP Business One? Sometimes other solutions are available that do not require the cost implications of a full-blown project?
<--- Score

24. Is there a Performance Baseline?
<--- Score

25. Are losses documented, analyzed, and remedial processes developed to prevent future losses?
<--- Score

26. How frequently do we track measures?
<--- Score

27. How is progress measured?
<--- Score

28. What measurements are possible, practicable and meaningful?
<--- Score

29. How to measure lifecycle phases?
<--- Score

30. What should be measured?
<--- Score

31. What about SAP Business One Analysis of results?
<--- Score

32. How will you measure your SAP Business One effectiveness?
<--- Score

33. What methods are feasible and acceptable to estimate the impact of reforms?
<--- Score

34. Why Measure?
<--- Score

35. Have the concerns of stakeholders to help identify and define potential barriers been obtained and analyzed?
<--- Score

36. What is measured?
<--- Score

37. How will effects be measured?
<--- Score

38. Among the SAP Business One product and service cost to be estimated, which is considered hardest to estimate?
<--- Score

39. How do your measurements capture actionable SAP Business One information for use in exceeding your customers expectations and securing your customers engagement?
<--- Score

40. What impact has the innovation of the ERP product (internet technology and configuration model) on the critical success factors?
<--- Score

41. Will SAP Business One have an impact on current business continuity, disaster recovery

processes and/or infrastructure?
<--- Score

42. Which customers cant participate in our SAP Business One domain because they lack skills, wealth, or convenient access to existing solutions?
<--- Score

43. What to measure and why?
<--- Score

44. Why identify and analyze stakeholders and their interests?
<--- Score

45. Is performance measured?
<--- Score

46. What evidence is there and what is measured?
<--- Score

47. What charts has the team used to display the components of variation in the process?
<--- Score

48. Is the solution cost-effective?
<--- Score

49. What has the team done to assure the stability and accuracy of the measurement process?
<--- Score

50. Have changes been properly/adequately analyzed for effect?
<--- Score

51. Are there measurements based on task performance?
<--- Score

52. What measurements are being captured?
<--- Score

53. One common pitfall is the lack of a comprehensive technology strategy that indicates the objectives of the CIM or ERP implementation: low cost or differentiation?
<--- Score

54. Is key measure data collection planned and executed, process variation displayed and communicated and performance baselined?
<--- Score

55. How can you measure SAP Business One in a systematic way?
<--- Score

56. Schedule Development, Feasibility Analysis, SAP Business One Management, Project Closings, Technique: Using the Critical Path Method
<--- Score

57. What are the agreed upon definitions of the high impact areas, defect(s), unit(s), and opportunities that will figure into the process capability metrics?
<--- Score

58. Is this an issue for analysis or intuition?
<--- Score

59. What are the key input variables? What are the key

process variables? What are the key output variables?
<--- Score

60. Is data collected on key measures that were identified?
<--- Score

61. What are our key indicators that you will measure, analyze and track?
<--- Score

62. How will your organization measure success?
<--- Score

63. Are we taking our company in the direction of better and revenue or cheaper and cost?
<--- Score

64. How is the value delivered by SAP Business One being measured?
<--- Score

65. Which Stakeholder Characteristics Are Analyzed?
<--- Score

66. Verify business objectives. Are they appropriate, and well-articulated?
<--- Score

67. Are process variation components displayed/ communicated using suitable charts, graphs, plots?
<--- Score

68. How do we focus on what is right -not who is right?
<--- Score

69. How do we do risk analysis of rare, cascading, catastrophic events?
<--- Score

70. What Relevant Entities could be measured?
<--- Score

71. What are your key SAP Business One organizational performance measures, including key short and longer-term financial measures?
<--- Score

72. Was a data collection plan established?
<--- Score

73. Does SAP Business One analysis show the relationships among important SAP Business One factors?
<--- Score

74. Does the SAP Business One task fit the client's priorities?
<--- Score

75. How large is the gap between current performance and the customer-specified (goal) performance?
<--- Score

76. What are measures?
<--- Score

77. Are the units of measure consistent?
<--- Score

78. How will success or failure be measured?
<--- Score

79. Do we have demonstrated experience providing oversight to keep ERP projects on target, scope, cost and time?
<--- Score

80. Is Process Variation Displayed/Communicated?
<--- Score

81. Who participated in the data collection for measurements?
<--- Score

82. Does SAP Business One systematically track and analyze outcomes for accountability and quality improvement?
<--- Score

83. Is it possible to estimate the impact of unanticipated complexity such as wrong or failed assumptions, feedback, etc. on proposed reforms?
<--- Score

84. How are you going to measure success?
<--- Score

85. How much does the ERP system cost?
<--- Score

86. How is Knowledge Management Measured?
<--- Score

87. Are key measures identified and agreed upon?
<--- Score

88. Do we aggressively reward and promote the people who have the biggest impact on creating excellent SAP Business One services/products?
<--- Score

89. When is Knowledge Management Measured?
<--- Score

90. How to measure variability?
<--- Score

91. Do staff have the necessary skills to collect, analyze, and report data?
<--- Score

92. Erp systems and management accounting change: opportunities or impacts?
<--- Score

93. Does the practice systematically track and analyze outcomes related for accountability and quality improvement?
<--- Score

94. Where is it measured?
<--- Score

95. How frequently do you track SAP Business One measures?
<--- Score

96. Verify business objectives. Are they appropriate, and well-articulated?
<--- Score

97. Why do measure/indicators matter?

<--- Score

98. Are high impact defects defined and identified in the stakeholder process?

<--- Score

99. What potential environmental factors impact the SAP Business One effort?

<--- Score

100. The approach of traditional SAP Business One works for detail complexity but is focused on a systematic approach rather than an understanding of the nature of systems themselves. what approach will permit us to deal with the kind of unpredictable emergent behaviors that dynamic complexity can introduce?

<--- Score

101. How do you identify and analyze stakeholders and their interests?

<--- Score

102. Why do the measurements/indicators matter?

<--- Score

103. Are the measurements objective?

<--- Score

104. Have all non-recommended alternatives been analyzed in sufficient detail?

<--- Score

105. Has the appropriate access to relevant data and analysis capability been granted?

<--- Score

106. What data was collected (past, present, future/ongoing)?
<--- Score

107. How are measurements made?
<--- Score

108. What is the right balance of time and resources between investigation, analysis, and discussion and dissemination?
<--- Score

109. Have you found any 'ground fruit' or 'low-hanging fruit' for immediate remedies to the gap in performance?
<--- Score

110. Do we effectively measure and reward individual and team performance?
<--- Score

111. Is long term and short term variability accounted for?
<--- Score

112. Business Case Analysis What Are Value Pockets?
<--- Score

113. How do you measure success?
<--- Score

114. Do ERP systems have any impact on business performance?

<--- Score

115. What particular quality tools did the team find helpful in establishing measurements?
<--- Score

116. Business Case Analysis; What Are Value Pockets?
<--- Score

117. Can We Measure the Return on Analysis?
<--- Score

118. Are you taking your company in the direction of better and revenue or cheaper and cost?
<--- Score

119. What are the types and number of measures to use?
<--- Score

Add up total points for this section:
_ _ _ _ _ = Total points for this section

Divided by: _ _ _ _ _ _ (number of statements answered) = _ _ _ _ _ _
Average score for this section

Transfer your score to the SAP Business One Index at the beginning of the Self-Assessment.

CRITERION #4: ANALYZE:

1. How does the organization define, manage, and improve its SAP Business One processes?
<--- Score

2. What finance, procurement and Human Resources business processes should be included in the scope of a erp solution?
<--- Score

3. Can we add value to the current SAP Business

One decision-making process (largely qualitative) by incorporating uncertainty modeling (more quantitative)?
<--- Score

4. How do you use SAP Business One data and information to support organizational decision making and innovation?
<--- Score

5. Was a cause-and-effect diagram used to explore the different types of causes (or sources of variation)?
<--- Score

6. Data Integrity, Is it SAP created?
<--- Score

7. What are our SAP Business One Processes?
<--- Score

8. What tools were used to narrow the list of possible causes?
<--- Score

9. How do you inventory and assess business processes as part of an erp evaluation?
<--- Score

10. Are best practices in an erp system simply a fancy term for process constraints?
<--- Score

11. How was the detailed process map generated, verified, and validated?
<--- Score

12. Do you, as a leader, bounce back quickly from setbacks?
<--- Score

13. How do you measure the Operational performance of your key work systems and processes, including productivity, cycle time, and other appropriate measures of process effectiveness, efficiency, and innovation?
<--- Score

14. What if separate islands of data were replaced with more integrated software ERP system created to serve and support multiple business functions and requirements?
<--- Score

15. What are the best opportunities for value improvement?
<--- Score

16. Have any additional benefits been identified that will result from closing all or most of the gaps?
<--- Score

17. Are ERP tools used for business process reengineering (BPR) or does BPR occur due to ERP implementation?
<--- Score

18. Was a detailed process map created to amplify critical steps of the 'as is' stakeholder process?
<--- Score

19. What are your current levels and trends in key SAP Business One measures or indicators

of product and process performance that are important to and directly serve your customers?
<--- Score

20. What other jobs or tasks affect the performance of the steps in the SAP Business One process?
<--- Score

21. What finance, procurement and human resources business processes should be included in the scope of our erp solution?
<--- Score

22. Did any value-added analysis or 'lean thinking' take place to identify some of the gaps shown on the 'as is' process map?
<--- Score

23. What will drive SAP Business One change?
<--- Score

24. What were the crucial 'moments of truth' on the process map?
<--- Score

25. Are gaps between current performance and the goal performance identified?
<--- Score

26. What does it mean to say that a company uses an erp system to automate their business processes across functional boundaries?
<--- Score

27. What conclusions were drawn from the team's

data collection and analysis? How did the team reach these conclusions?

<--- Score

28. How well do the existing business processes work and support our operations?

<--- Score

29. Record-keeping requirements flow from the records needed as inputs, outputs, controls and for transformation of a SAP Business One process. ask yourself: are the records needed as inputs to the SAP Business One process available?

<--- Score

30. Were Pareto charts (or similar) used to portray the 'heavy hitters' (or key sources of variation)?

<--- Score

31. Is the SAP Business One process severely broken such that a re-design is necessary?

<--- Score

32. What quality tools were used to get through the analyze phase?

<--- Score

33. What are the business drivers?

<--- Score

34. Did any additional data need to be collected?

<--- Score

35. Were any designed experiments used to generate additional insight into the data analysis?

<--- Score

36. An organizationally feasible system request is one that considers the mission, goals and objectives of the organization. key questions are: is the solution request practical and will it solve a problem or take advantage of an opportunity to achieve company goals?
<--- Score

37. Identify an operational issue in your organization. for example, could a particular task be done more quickly or more efficiently?
<--- Score

38. What tools were used to generate the list of possible causes?
<--- Score

39. Teaches and consults on quality process improvement, project management, and accelerated SAP Business One techniques
<--- Score

40. What did the team gain from developing a sub-process map?
<--- Score

41. Were there any improvement opportunities identified from the process analysis?
<--- Score

42. What is the cost of poor quality as supported by the team's analysis?
<--- Score

43. How do mission and objectives affect the SAP

Business One processes of our organization?
<--- Score

44. How do we promote understanding that opportunity for improvement is not criticism of the status quo, or the people who created the status quo?
<--- Score

45. What are the disruptive SAP Business One technologies that enable our organization to radically change our business processes?
<--- Score

46. A compounding model resolution with available relevant data can often provide insight towards a solution methodology; which SAP Business One models, tools and techniques are necessary?
<--- Score

47. Do your employees have the opportunity to do what they do best everyday?
<--- Score

48. What controls do we have in place to protect data?
<--- Score

49. What does the data say about the performance of the stakeholder process?
<--- Score

50. Have the problem and goal statements been updated to reflect the additional knowledge gained from the analyze phase?
<--- Score

51. Think about some of the processes you undertake within your organization. which do you own?

<--- Score

52. What other organizational variables, such as reward systems or communication systems, affect the performance of this SAP Business One process?

<--- Score

53. Think about the functions involved in your SAP Business One project. what processes flow from these functions?

<--- Score

54. What successful thing are we doing today that may be blinding us to new growth opportunities?

<--- Score

55. What are the revised rough estimates of the financial savings/opportunity for SAP Business One improvements?

<--- Score

56. Designing ERP Systems: Should Business Processes or ERP Software Be Changed?

<--- Score

57. How are ERP systems included in business process risk management and what controls are adopted?

<--- Score

58. When conducting a business process

reengineering study, what should we look for when trying to identify business processes to change?

<--- Score

59. Is Data and process analysis, root cause analysis and quantifying the gap/opportunity in place?

<--- Score

60. Where is the data coming from to measure compliance?

<--- Score

61. What were the financial benefits resulting from any 'ground fruit or low-hanging fruit' (quick fixes)?

<--- Score

62. No single business unit responsible for enterprise data?

<--- Score

63. Is the gap/opportunity displayed and communicated in financial terms?

<--- Score

64. Is the suppliers process defined and controlled?

<--- Score

65. Is the performance gap determined?

<--- Score

66. What is Master Data?

<--- Score

67. How does the traditional systems development

life cycle differ from the ERP information systems design and implementation process?

<--- Score

68. How often will data be collected for measures?

<--- Score

69. How is the way you as the leader think and process information affecting your organizational culture?

<--- Score

70. Do our leaders quickly bounce back from setbacks?

<--- Score

71. What are your current levels and trends in key measures or indicators of SAP Business One product and process performance that are important to and directly serve your customers? how do these results compare with the performance of your competitors and other organizations with similar offerings?

<--- Score

72. Is erp system a good example of a data warehouse?

<--- Score

73. What is the technical model for interfacing (e.g. messaging, data warehouse, email, robotics, data download, etc.)?

<--- Score

74. What process should we select for improvement?

<--- Score

Add up total points for this section:
_ _ _ _ _ = Total points for this section

Divided by: _ _ _ _ _ _ (number of
statements answered) = _ _ _ _ _ _
Average score for this section

Transfer your score to the SAP Business
One Index at the beginning of the Self-
Assessment.

CRITERION #5: IMPROVE:

INTENT: Develop a practical solution.
Innovate, establish and test the
solution and to measure the results.

In my belief, the answer to this
question is clearly defined:

5 Strongly Agree

4 Agree

3 Neutral

2 Disagree

1 Strongly Disagree

1. How can we improve SAP Business One?
<--- Score

2. What tools were used to evaluate the potential
solutions?
<--- Score

**3. How do you manage and improve your SAP
Business One work systems to deliver customer**

value and achieve organizational success and sustainability?

<--- Score

4. Why improve in the first place?

<--- Score

5. How do we improve productivity?

<--- Score

6. How do we measure risk?

<--- Score

7. How Do We Link Measurement and Risk?

<--- Score

8. Knowledge problem: How to determine the optimal methodology for ERP projects?

<--- Score

9. How could extended ERP components help improve business operations at your organization?

<--- Score

10. Does the goal represent a desired result that can be measured?

<--- Score

11. What communications are necessary to support the implementation of the solution?

<--- Score

12. Many divisions of organizations seek decentralized financial control. How can an ERP system be implemented to ensure local financial decision making and control?

<--- Score

13. What actually has to improve and by how much?
<--- Score

14. What does the 'should be' process map/design look like?
<--- Score

15. Describe the design of the pilot and what tests were conducted, if any?
<--- Score

16. Which ERP modules could help a company develop new products?
<--- Score

17. What evaluation strategy is needed and what needs to be done to assure its implementation and use?
<--- Score

18. What were your companys total expenditures to integrate neutral file formats and/or develop intersystem connectivity into your CAD, CAM, CAE, PDM, or ERP systems?
<--- Score

19. Are improved process ('should be') maps modified based on pilot data and analysis?
<--- Score

20. What improvements have been achieved?
<--- Score

21. How can erp improve your companys business performance?
<--- Score

22. Is the solution technically practical?
<--- Score

23. In the past few months, what is the smallest change we have made that has had the biggest positive result? What was it about that small change that produced the large return?
<--- Score

24. Who will be responsible for documenting the SAP Business One requirements in detail?
<--- Score

25. What is the SAP Business One sustainability risk?
<--- Score

26. To what extent does management recognize SAP Business One as a tool to increase the results?
<--- Score

27. What is the team's contingency plan for potential problems occurring in implementation?
<--- Score

28. What tools were used to tap into the creativity and encourage 'outside the box' thinking?
<--- Score

29. How will we know that a change is improvement?
<--- Score

30. What is the perceived risk of erp projects?

<--- Score

31. Why might varying hurdle rates be applicable for this decision?
<--- Score

32. Do we combine technical expertise with business knowledge and SAP Business One Key topics include lifecycles, development approaches, requirements and how to make a business case?
<--- Score

33. Is Supporting SAP Business One documentation required?
<--- Score

34. What do we want to improve?
<--- Score

35. Is there a cost/benefit analysis of optimal solution(s)?
<--- Score

36. Is a contingency plan established?
<--- Score

37. How did the team generate the list of possible solutions?
<--- Score

38. Which ERP modules could help your company develop new products?
<--- Score

39. Were any criteria developed to assist the team in testing and evaluating potential solutions?

<--- Score

40. How significant is the improvement in the eyes of the end user?
<--- Score

41. What resources are required for the improvement effort?
<--- Score

42. How much time and money is it truly going to take to fully implement ERP as a business solution, not just a piece of software?
<--- Score

43. Is the optimal solution selected based on testing and analysis?
<--- Score

44. Are we using SAP Business One to communicate information about our Cybersecurity Risk Management programs including the effectiveness of those programs to stakeholders, including boards, investors, auditors, and insurers?
<--- Score

45. Can the solution be designed and implemented within an acceptable time period?
<--- Score

46. Who controls key decisions that will be made?
<--- Score

47. Are we Assessing SAP Business One and Risk?
<--- Score

48. If you could go back in time five years, what decision would you make differently? What is your best guess as to what decision you're making today you might regret five years from now?
<--- Score

49. Is the measure understandable to a variety of people?
<--- Score

50. What error proofing will be done to address some of the discrepancies observed in the 'as is' process?
<--- Score

51. What were the underlying assumptions on the cost-benefit analysis?
<--- Score

52. Do we cover the five essential competencies-Communication, Collaboration,Innovation, Adaptability, and Leadership that improve an organization's ability to leverage the new SAP Business One in a volatile global economy?
<--- Score

53. How will you know that you have improved?
<--- Score

54. Are the best solutions selected?
<--- Score

55. Who controls the risk?
<--- Score

56. What is SAP Business One's impact on utilizing the

best solution(s)?

<--- Score

57. Is a solution implementation plan established, including schedule/work breakdown structure, resources, risk management plan, cost/budget, and control plan?

<--- Score

58. How can we improve performance?

<--- Score

59. What are the implications of this decision 10 minutes, 10 months, and 10 years from now?

<--- Score

60. Is there a high likelihood that any recommendations will achieve their intended results?

<--- Score

61. What tools do you use once you have decided on a SAP Business One strategy and more importantly how do you choose?

<--- Score

62. Explorations of the frontiers of SAP Business One will help you build influence, improve SAP Business One, optimize decision making, and sustain change

<--- Score

63. What does this integration solution include?

<--- Score

64. What is the anticipated lifecycle for the ERP solution?

<--- Score

65. How important is time-to-market for added functionality or new solutions?
<--- Score

66. Who are the people involved in developing and implementing SAP Business One?
<--- Score

67. What went well, what should change, what can improve?
<--- Score

68. What to do with the results or outcomes of measurements?
<--- Score

69. How to Improve?
<--- Score

70. How will the group know that the solution worked?
<--- Score

71. How will the team or the process owner(s) monitor the implementation plan to see that it is working as intended?
<--- Score

72. How can integrating SCM, CRM, and ERP help improve business operations at your organization?
<--- Score

73. Who will be responsible for making the decisions to include or exclude requested changes once SAP

Business One is underway?

<--- Score

74. What is the approach for your organization to manage organizational change needed to implement and operate a new ERP solution?

<--- Score

75. How can skill-level changes improve SAP Business One?

<--- Score

76. What are (or were) the top risks identified for erp upgrade projects?

<--- Score

77. What is the implementation plan?

<--- Score

78. What should a proof of concept or pilot accomplish?

<--- Score

79. How do you measure progress and evaluate training effectiveness?

<--- Score

80. How will you measure the results?

<--- Score

81. Who will be using the results of the measurement activities?

<--- Score

82. How do we decide how much to remunerate an employee?

<--- Score

83. How does erp improve the business?
<--- Score

84. What needs improvement?
<--- Score

85. How could core ERP components help improve business operations at your organization?
<--- Score

86. Are new and improved process ('should be') maps developed?
<--- Score

87. How does the team improve its work?
<--- Score

88. Is the implementation plan designed?
<--- Score

89. At what point will vulnerability assessments be performed once SAP Business One is put into production (e.g., ongoing Risk Management after implementation)?
<--- Score

90. What tools were most useful during the improve phase?
<--- Score

91. How do we measure improved SAP Business One service perception, and satisfaction?
<--- Score

92. How can an ERP system improve Supply Chain Management by enabling firms to participate in on-line marketplaces?

<--- Score

93. For estimation problems, how do you develop an estimation statement?

<--- Score

94. How does the solution remove the key sources of issues discovered in the analyze phase?

<--- Score

95. Was a pilot designed for the proposed solution(s)?

<--- Score

96. What lessons, if any, from a pilot were incorporated into the design of the full-scale solution?

<--- Score

97. Is there a small-scale pilot for proposed improvement(s)? What conclusions were drawn from the outcomes of a pilot?

<--- Score

98. How do you improve your likelihood of success ?

<--- Score

99. What attendant changes will need to be made to ensure that the solution is successful?

<--- Score

100. Risk factors: what are the characteristics of SAP Business One that make it risky?

<--- Score

101. How do we Improve SAP Business One service perception, and satisfaction?
<--- Score

102. What is the magnitude of the improvements?
<--- Score

103. How will you know when its improved?
<--- Score

104. How do we go about Comparing SAP Business One approaches/solutions?
<--- Score

105. For decision problems, how do you develop a decision statement?
<--- Score

106. How important is the completion of a recognized college or graduate-level degree program in the hiring decision?
<--- Score

107. How do the SAP Business One results compare with the performance of your competitors and other organizations with similar offerings?
<--- Score

108. Are there any constraints (technical, political, cultural, or otherwise) that would inhibit certain solutions?
<--- Score

109. What is the risk?
<--- Score

110. Is pilot data collected and analyzed?
<--- Score

111. What can we do to improve?
<--- Score

112. Risk events: what are the things that could go wrong?
<--- Score

113. How do we keep improving SAP Business One?
<--- Score

114. Are possible solutions generated and tested?
<--- Score

Add up total points for this section:
_ _ _ _ _ = Total points for this section

Divided by: _ _ _ _ _ _ (number of statements answered) = _ _ _ _ _ _
Average score for this section

Transfer your score to the SAP Business One Index at the beginning of the Self-Assessment.

CRITERION #6: CONTROL:

INTENT: Implement the practical solution. Maintain the performance and correct possible complications.

In my belief, the answer to this question is clearly defined:

5 Strongly Agree

4 Agree

3 Neutral

2 Disagree

1 Strongly Disagree

1. Against what alternative is success being measured?
<--- Score

2. What are the critical parameters to watch?
<--- Score

3. Are new process steps, standards, and documentation ingrained into normal operations?

<--- Score

4. What is the recommended frequency of auditing?
<--- Score

5. What is the control/monitoring plan?
<--- Score

6. In the case of a SAP Business One project, the criteria for the audit derive from implementation objectives. an audit of a SAP Business One project involves assessing whether the recommendations outlined for implementation have been met. in other words, can we track that any SAP Business One project is implemented as planned, and is it working?
<--- Score

7. Do the decisions we make today help people and the planet tomorrow?
<--- Score

8. How do our controls stack up?
<--- Score

9. Is there documentation that will support the successful operation of the improvement?
<--- Score

10. What is your theory of human motivation, and how does your compensation plan fit with that view?
<--- Score

11. How important is Control to your organization?
<--- Score

12. Does SAP Business One appropriately measure and monitor risk?
<--- Score

13. Does job training on the documented procedures need to be part of the process team's education and training?
<--- Score

14. Is there a standardized process?
<--- Score

15. What quality tools were useful in the control phase?
<--- Score

16. What are some good low cost Material Requirement Planning MRP packages for small manufacturers?
<--- Score

17. What should the next improvement project be that is related to SAP Business One?
<--- Score

18. Measure, Monitor and Predict SAP Business One Activities to Optimize Operations and Profitably, and Enhance Outcomes
<--- Score

19. What do we stand for--and what are we against?
<--- Score

20. Are documented procedures clear and easy to follow for the operators?

<--- Score

21. What plans do you have for future developments/implementation?
<--- Score

22. What other areas of the group might benefit from the SAP Business One team's improvements, knowledge, and learning?
<--- Score

23. How do you select, collect, align, and integrate SAP Business One data and information for tracking daily operations and overall organizational performance, including progress relative to strategic objectives and action plans?
<--- Score

24. Strategic planning -SAP Business One relations
<--- Score

25. Who controls critical resources?
<--- Score

26. Implementation Planning- is a pilot needed to test the changes before a full roll out occurs?
<--- Score

27. Are pertinent alerts monitored, analyzed and distributed to appropriate personnel?
<--- Score

28. Who is the SAP Business One process owner?
<--- Score

29. Have new or revised work instructions resulted?

<--- Score

30. Is knowledge gained on process shared and institutionalized?
<--- Score

31. Works with enterprise resources planning (ERP) systems?
<--- Score

32. How will new or emerging customer needs/ requirements be checked/communicated to orient the process toward meeting the new specifications and continually reducing variation?
<--- Score

33. Is reporting being used or needed?
<--- Score

34. How will the process owner verify improvement in present and future sigma levels, process capabilities?
<--- Score

35. What are the key elements of your SAP Business One performance improvement system, including your evaluation, organizational learning, and innovation processes?
<--- Score

36. Will existing staff require re-training, for example, to learn new business processes?
<--- Score

37. Is there a SAP Business One Communication plan covering who needs to get what information when?

<--- Score

38. What are the known security controls?
<--- Score

39. How likely is the current SAP Business One plan to come in on schedule or on budget?
<--- Score

40. What are we attempting to measure/monitor?
<--- Score

41. How will the process owner and team be able to hold the gains?
<--- Score

42. Do we monitor the SAP Business One decisions made and fine tune them as they evolve?
<--- Score

43. Is there a control plan in place for sustaining improvements (short and long-term)?
<--- Score

44. Why Cash Flow Planning?
<--- Score

45. Are suggested corrective/restorative actions indicated on the response plan for known causes to problems that might surface?
<--- Score

46. What is the relationship between enterprise asset management eam systems and enterprise resource planning erp systems within asset intensive organizations?

<--- Score

47. SAP Business One in management -Strategic planning
<--- Score

48. Do we have demonstrated experience planning ERP data warehouse and reporting projects?
<--- Score

49. Were the planned controls working?
<--- Score

50. Where do ideas that reach policy makers and planners as proposals for SAP Business One strengthening and reform actually originate?
<--- Score

51. What should we measure to verify effectiveness gains?
<--- Score

52. How do distribution resource planning (DRP) and enterprise resource planning (ERP) differ?
<--- Score

53. Do the SAP Business One decisions we make today help people and the planet tomorrow?
<--- Score

54. What can you control?
<--- Score

55. What is your quality control system?
<--- Score

56. Can SAP Business One be learned?
<--- Score

57. What is the difference between a warehouse management system wms and an enterprise resource planning erp system?
<--- Score

58. Are there documented procedures?
<--- Score

59. Who has control over resources?
<--- Score

60. Does a troubleshooting guide exist or is it needed?
<--- Score

61. Whats the best design framework for SAP Business One organization now that, in a post industrial-age if the top-down, command and control model is no longer relevant?
<--- Score

62. How can we best use all of our knowledge repositories to enhance learning and sharing?
<--- Score

63. Is a response plan established and deployed?
<--- Score

64. Is there a recommended audit plan for routine surveillance inspections of SAP Business One's gains?
<--- Score

65. Has the improved process and its steps been standardized?

<--- Score

66. Are operating procedures consistent?
<--- Score

67. Do you regularly review existing interfaces as well as planning future interfaces between ERP applications and other applications within the organization?
<--- Score

68. Who will be in control?
<--- Score

69. How will input, process, and output variables be checked to detect for sub-optimal conditions?
<--- Score

70. Control: how much centralization, drill-down visibility?
<--- Score

71. What are your results for key measures or indicators of the accomplishment of your SAP Business One strategy and action plans, including building and strengthening core competencies?
<--- Score

72. If the system is a local one, have you had discussions with the LSP about migration or integration with the NCRS and what migration/ integration plans have been identified/agreed?
<--- Score

73. How might the group capture best practices and lessons learned so as to leverage improvements?

<--- Score

74. How can enterprise resource planning facilitate organizational transformation?
<--- Score

75. Does the response plan contain a definite closed loop continual improvement scheme (e.g., plan-do-check-act)?
<--- Score

76. What other systems, operations, processes, and infrastructures (hiring practices, staffing, training, incentives/rewards, metrics/dashboards/scorecards, etc.) need updates, additions, changes, or deletions in order to facilitate knowledge transfer and improvements?
<--- Score

77. Does the SAP Business One performance meet the customer's requirements?
<--- Score

78. Is there a transfer of ownership and knowledge to process owner and process team tasked with the responsibilities.
<--- Score

79. How will report readings be checked to effectively monitor performance?
<--- Score

80. How will the day-to-day responsibilities for monitoring and continual improvement be transferred from the improvement team to the process owner?

<--- Score

81. How do you encourage people to take control and responsibility?
<--- Score

82. Do you monitor the effectiveness of your SAP Business One activities?
<--- Score

83. Will any special training be provided for results interpretation?
<--- Score

84. What key inputs and outputs are being measured on an ongoing basis?
<--- Score

85. Is new knowledge gained imbedded in the response plan?
<--- Score

86. What should we measure to verify efficiency gains?
<--- Score

87. Are controls in place and consistently applied?
<--- Score

88. Is there a documented and implemented monitoring plan?
<--- Score

89. Is a response plan in place for when the input, process, or output measures indicate an 'out-of-control' condition?

<--- Score

90. What is our theory of human motivation, and how does our compensation plan fit with that view?
<--- Score

91. Were the planned controls in place?
<--- Score

92. Why is change control necessary?
<--- Score

93. How do controls support value?
<--- Score

Add up total points for this section:
_ _ _ _ _ = Total points for this section

Divided by: _ _ _ _ _ _ (number of statements answered) = _ _ _ _ _ _
Average score for this section

Transfer your score to the SAP Business One Index at the beginning of the Self-Assessment.

CRITERION #7: SUSTAIN:

INTENT: Retain the benefits.

In my belief, the answer to this
question is clearly defined:

5 Strongly Agree

4 Agree

3 Neutral

2 Disagree

1 Strongly Disagree

1. What is an unauthorized commitment?
<--- Score

2. Among our stronger employees, how many see
themselves at the company in three years? How
many would leave for a 10 percent raise from another
company?
<--- Score

3. If we weren't already in this business, would we
enter it today? And if not, what are we going to do

about it?

<--- Score

4. Do companies that implement erp systems see a decent adoption?

<--- Score

5. What potential megatrends could make our business model obsolete?

<--- Score

6. How do we Lead with SAP Business One in Mind?

<--- Score

7. Do we have the right capabilities and capacities?

<--- Score

8. How do I stay inspired?

<--- Score

9. Are we paying enough attention to the partners our company depends on to succeed?

<--- Score

10. When and why did erp systems begin specializing by industry verticals?

<--- Score

11. Political -is anyone trying to undermine this project?

<--- Score

12. What is the relation between dependencies and the strength of the relation between methodology and ERP project outcomes?

<--- Score

13. What do you think is the most common term used by business people to describe their erp system?
<--- Score

14. What current systems have to be understood and/or changed?
<--- Score

15. Is your ERP keeping pace?
<--- Score

16. What is the system used for?
<--- Score

17. What is the relation between project category and the strength of the relation between methodology and ERP project outcomes?
<--- Score

18. How long will it take to change?
<--- Score

19. Is a SAP Business One Team Work effort in place?
<--- Score

20. Whose voice (department, ethnic group, women, older workers, etc) might you have missed hearing from in your company, and how might you amplify this voice to create positive momentum for your business?
<--- Score

21. What is the best erp system to manage contract approval forms?

<--- Score

22. Who is responsible for errors?
<--- Score

23. Why is the design and selection of ERP architecture crucial for the implementation project?
<--- Score

24. Discuss the criteria for selecting ERP vendors. Which is the most important criteria and why?
<--- Score

25. How do you determine the key elements that affect SAP Business One workforce satisfaction? how are these elements determined for different workforce groups and segments?
<--- Score

26. Instead of going to current contacts for new ideas, what if you reconnected with dormant contacts-- the people you used to know? If you were going reactivate a dormant tie, who would it be?
<--- Score

27. What are internal and external SAP Business One relations?
<--- Score

28. If we do not follow, then how to lead?
<--- Score

29. Is there any reason to believe the opposite of my current belief?
<--- Score

30. What is the most important feature that an ERP must have in terms of Human Resource?
<--- Score

31. How do organisations achieve competitive advantage even if they use the same ERP systems?
<--- Score

32. How is supporting a BI environment different from supporting an ERP implementation?
<--- Score

33. How do we provide a safe environment -physically and emotionally?
<--- Score

34. How can we become the company that would put us out of business?
<--- Score

35. What knowledge, skills and characteristics mark a good SAP Business One project manager?
<--- Score

36. What do you already have?
<--- Score

37. Is it economical; do we have the time and money?
<--- Score

38. Who sets the SAP Business One standards?
<--- Score

39. Which Consultants Do ERP Systems?

<--- Score

40. Whom among your colleagues do you trust, and for what?
<--- Score

41. How many FTEs are supporting the ERP system?
<--- Score

42. Do we underestimate the customer's journey?
<--- Score

43. How to deal with SAP Business One Changes?
<--- Score

44. What would have to be true for the option on the table to be the best possible choice?
<--- Score

45. What role does communication play in the success or failure of a SAP Business One project?
<--- Score

46. How can you negotiate SAP Business One successfully with a stubborn boss, an irate client, or a deceitful coworker?
<--- Score

47. What is the role of change management in the ERP life cycle?
<--- Score

48. Which SAP Business One goals are the most important?
<--- Score

49. How does it help me?
<--- Score

50. The Financial Accounting module is often the first module to be implemented within an ERP system. Why do many companies start with the Financial Accounting module?
<--- Score

51. What information is critical to our organization that our executives are ignoring?
<--- Score

52. What is the estimated value of the project?
<--- Score

53. Is a single department responsible for overseeing the governance of the ERP system?
<--- Score

54. What is your BATNA (best alternative to a negotiated agreement)?
<--- Score

55. Change company to follow software ?
<--- Score

56. How will we ensure we get what we expected?
<--- Score

57. The Cloud is offering many benefits to businesses of all sizes and across all industries, but is it right for you?
<--- Score

58. Who do we want our customers to become?
<--- Score

59. Can we maintain our growth without detracting from the factors that have contributed to our success?
<--- Score

60. How will you know that the SAP Business One project has been successful?
<--- Score

61. If we got kicked out and the board brought in a new CEO, what would he do?
<--- Score

62. Who are the ERP Companies?
<--- Score

63. Do you want to grow your business overseas?
<--- Score

64. Why is it important to have senior management support for a SAP Business One project?
<--- Score

65. How do we engage the workforce, in addition to satisfying them?
<--- Score

66. What happens if you do not have enough funding?
<--- Score

67. Whats different from SAP Business One and R

3?
<--- Score

68. How do you quantify the potential business benefits of a future ERP implementation?
<--- Score

69. Will erp fit the ways we do business?
<--- Score

70. Why should we adopt a SAP Business One framework?
<--- Score

71. Who will manage the integration of tools?
<--- Score

72. How many person months are involved to roll out a generic erp system?
<--- Score

73. How do senior leaders deploy your organizations vision and values through your leadership system, to the workforce, to key suppliers and partners, and to customers and other stakeholders, as appropriate?
<--- Score

74. What is ERP Success?
<--- Score

75. What is the ideal percentage of revenue that a company should spend on an erp system?
<--- Score

76. With ERP implementations why would an

auditor get involved?
<--- Score

77. Who, on the executive team or the board, has spoken to a customer recently?
<--- Score

78. How do you determine ROI on COE?
<--- Score

79. Password change policies and timelines for the erp system and associated third party products can be managed from the organizations security management system?
<--- Score

80. Who will determine interim and final deadlines?
<--- Score

81. What are top SaaS ERP companies that target SMBs?
<--- Score

82. Think about the kind of project structure that would be appropriate for your SAP Business One project. should it be formal and complex, or can it be less formal and relatively simple?
<--- Score

83. How can the use of ERP systems remove information or functional silos in organizations?
<--- Score

84. Are we changing as fast as the world around us?
<--- Score

85. What do you feel are the factors that have contributed most to the success of your project?
<--- Score

86. What is something you believe that nearly no one agrees with you on?
<--- Score

87. If our company went out of business tomorrow, would anyone who doesn't get a paycheck here care?
<--- Score

88. What were the conditions at our organization that made an ERP system desirable?
<--- Score

89. What is different with integration framework as platform?
<--- Score

90. SAP Business One Service Sales Supply Chain, Procurement, Distribution
<--- Score

91. Design Thinking: Integrating Innovation, SAP Business One, and Brand Value
<--- Score

92. Standing on the Shoulders of Giants: Are ERP success factors relevant for EDRMS Implementation?
<--- Score

93. How is business? Why?
<--- Score

94. Have new benefits been realized?

<--- Score

95. Can our administrative systems support its business goals and objectives?

<--- Score

96. Whats the best way to add new features to an old erp system?

<--- Score

97. Is there any existing SAP Business One governance structure?

<--- Score

98. What are the benefits of hosted cloud ERP software?

<--- Score

99. How do we keep the momentum going?

<--- Score

100. What is the best open source erp system for a middle size business?

<--- Score

101. Do we say no to customers for no reason?

<--- Score

102. What are the rules and assumptions my industry operates under? What if the opposite were true?

<--- Score

103. Does the firm have a single, company-wide ERP system that can easily be linked to its key

suppliers and customers information systems?
<--- Score

104. What is the purpose of SAP Business One in relation to the mission?
<--- Score

105. Can ERP meet the demands?
<--- Score

106. What are several key things companies should do to avoid ERP systems failures?
<--- Score

107. Who will use it?
<--- Score

108. In a project to restructure SAP Business One outcomes, which stakeholders would you involve?
<--- Score

109. How Do We Know if We Are Successful?
<--- Score

110. Is the impact that SAP Business One has shown?
<--- Score

111. Did my employees make progress today?
<--- Score

112. Is there a limit on the number of users in SAP Business One ?
<--- Score

113. What are the top 3 things at the forefront of our SAP Business One agendas for the next 3

years?
<--- Score

114. What are the challenges?
<--- Score

115. What will be the consequences to the stakeholder (financial, reputation etc) if SAP Business One does not go ahead or fails to deliver the objectives?
<--- Score

116. Has implementation been effective in reaching specified objectives?
<--- Score

117. What business benefits will SAP Business One goals deliver if achieved?
<--- Score

118. What are the short and long-term SAP Business One goals?
<--- Score

119. Do you keep 50% of your time unscheduled?
<--- Score

120. Why don't our customers like us?
<--- Score

121. How do we maintain SAP Business One's Integrity?
<--- Score

122. What are the potential consequences that erp systems may present for management

accountants?
<--- Score

123. Does the firm have a single, company-wide ERP system, linking all functional areas?
<--- Score

124. Which models, tools and techniques are necessary?
<--- Score

125. Have you properly acknowledged all amendments?
<--- Score

126. Cloud vs. on-premise vs. hybrid, which one is better and why?
<--- Score

127. What are the gaps in my knowledge and experience?
<--- Score

128. What are the Key enablers to make this SAP Business One move?
<--- Score

129. Ask yourself: how would we do this work if we only had one staff member to do it?
<--- Score

130. What is our competitive advantage?
<--- Score

131. What is the best web based erp system out there?

<--- Score

132. How do we accomplish our long range SAP Business One goals?
<--- Score

133. Who will be responsible for deciding whether SAP Business One goes ahead or not after the initial investigations?
<--- Score

134. Could you illustrate what HR/HCM functionality you desire from the relevant HCM module of the new CPM/Cloud ERP system?
<--- Score

135. How likely is it that a customer would recommend our company to a friend or colleague?
<--- Score

136. How do we ensure that implementations of SAP Business One products are done in a way that ensures safety?
<--- Score

137. Is our strategy driving our strategy? Or is the way in which we allocate resources driving our strategy?
<--- Score

138. Do we have the right people on the bus?
<--- Score

139. How much does SAP Business One help?
<--- Score

140. What new services of functionality will be

implemented next with SAP Business One ?
<--- Score

141. What counts that we are not counting?
<--- Score

142. Who do we think the world wants us to be?
<--- Score

143. Best practices: how willing to embrace?
<--- Score

144. Which functions and people interact with the supplier and or customer?
<--- Score

145. What are the critical steps of the ERP project cycle?
<--- Score

146. What is the best erp system for a new small business company?
<--- Score

147. Will it be accepted by users?
<--- Score

148. Who else should we help?
<--- Score

149. Is reviewing policies and procedures considered a third-party service?
<--- Score

150. Are the assumptions believable and achievable?

<--- Score

151. Does the ERP system interface to other operational systems in use?
<--- Score

152. Are you satisfied with your current role? If not, what is missing from it?
<--- Score

153. What trouble can we get into?
<--- Score

154. How can we incorporate support to ensure safe and effective use of SAP Business One into the services that we provide?
<--- Score

155. How you manage your Shipment Tracking in eCommerce through the SAP Business One SAP B1?
<--- Score

156. What is the cancellation rate of ERP within a year after the deal closes?
<--- Score

157. What Are the Challenges of Implementing an ERP System?
<--- Score

158. Schedule -can it be done in the given time?
<--- Score

159. What is the basic ERP Life Cycle?
<--- Score

160. Why are SAP Business One skills important?

<--- Score

161. What erp systems are ecommerce companies using?

<--- Score

162. Are there SAP Business One Models?

<--- Score

163. Who is responsible for ensuring appropriate resources (time, people and money) are allocated to SAP Business One?

<--- Score

164. Is the SAP Business One organization completing tasks effectively and efficiently?

<--- Score

165. Will there be any necessary staff changes (redundancies or new hires)?

<--- Score

166. What is our question?

<--- Score

167. How Do We Create Buy-in?

<--- Score

168. What are specific SAP Business One Rules to follow?

<--- Score

169. Do you have any supplemental information to add to this checklist?

<--- Score

170. If no one would ever find out about my accomplishments, how would I lead differently?
<--- Score

171. What assessment tools are you using on the system?
<--- Score

172. Who uses our product in ways we never expected?
<--- Score

173. Which individuals, teams or departments will be involved in SAP Business One?
<--- Score

174. Were lessons learned captured and communicated?
<--- Score

175. How do ERP systems supporting Supply Chain Management and Customer Relationship Management provide a foundation for eBusiness?
<--- Score

176. Are new benefits received and understood?
<--- Score

177. Cloud, On-Premise, or Hybrid: Which Operational Platform Best Suits Your Project?
<--- Score

178. Does ERP build a better business?
<--- Score

179. What are we challenging, in the sense that Mac challenged the PC or Dove tackled the Beauty Myth?
<--- Score

180. Is there undisputed evidence that erp increases business productivity and profitability is there any drawback such as flexibility innovation etc?
<--- Score

181. What is the overall business strategy?
<--- Score

182. Who are the key stakeholders?
<--- Score

183. Is the synchronization in one direction or bi-directional (update anywhere)?
<--- Score

184. Are assumptions made in SAP Business One stated explicitly?
<--- Score

185. Which start ups are working on ERP SaaS?
<--- Score

186. What Are the Modules of an ERP System?
<--- Score

187. The business environment is changing faster than ever before. Is your ERP keeping pace?
<--- Score

188. What makes ERP systems so special and so

important in accounting education?
<--- Score

189. R/3 Enterprise or MySAP ERP ?
<--- Score

190. What Should You Worry About ?
<--- Score

191. Who is the main stakeholder, with ultimate responsibility for driving SAP Business One forward?
<--- Score

192. What is our formula for success in SAP Business One ?
<--- Score

193. Can the organization's administrative systems support its business goals and objectives?
<--- Score

194. If our customer were my grandmother, would I tell her to buy what we're selling?
<--- Score

195. How are we doing compared to our industry?
<--- Score

196. What is it like to work for me?
<--- Score

197. Are we making progress? and are we making progress as SAP Business One leaders?
<--- Score

198. What would I recommend my friend do if he were

facing this dilemma?

<--- Score

199. What one word do we want to own in the minds of our customers, employees, and partners?

<--- Score

200. What Are the Benefits of an ERP System?

<--- Score

201. What are all of our SAP Business One domains and what do they do?

<--- Score

202. What did we miss in the interview for the worst hire we ever made?

<--- Score

203. What is the funding source for this project?

<--- Score

204. How much contingency will be available in the budget?

<--- Score

205. What should we stop doing?

<--- Score

206. Why is it important?

<--- Score

207. Is maximizing SAP Business One protection the same as minimizing SAP Business One loss?

<--- Score

208. What are the success criteria that will indicate

that SAP Business One objectives have been met and the benefits delivered?
<--- Score

209. What are some new service areas that are complimentary to ERP consulting yet get away from the reliance on software publishers and their margins?
<--- Score

210. Do the values of ERP project outcomes change as a function of the applied methodology?
<--- Score

211. How do we go about Securing SAP Business One?
<--- Score

212. What return can your company expect from its ERP investment?
<--- Score

213. Are the criteria for selecting recommendations stated?
<--- Score

214. Do you have a vision statement?
<--- Score

215. What kind of crime could a potential new hire have committed that would not only not disqualify him/her from being hired by our organization, but would actually indicate that he/she might be a particularly good fit?
<--- Score

216. What is joint and several liability?
<--- Score

217. Why should people listen to you?
<--- Score

218. You may have created your customer policies at a time when you lacked resources, technology wasn't up-to-snuff, or low service levels were the industry norm. Have those circumstances changed?
<--- Score

219. Expanding ERP Application Software: Buy, Lease, Outsource, or Write Your Own?
<--- Score

220. If there were zero limitations, what would we do differently?
<--- Score

221. What sources do you use to gather information for a SAP Business One study?
<--- Score

222. What are the main factors in choosing an erp system for manufacturers?
<--- Score

223. Will I get fired?
<--- Score

224. What happens when a new employee joins the organization?
<--- Score

225. How do we foster the skills, knowledge, talents, attributes, and characteristics we want to have?

<--- Score

226. Is SAP Business One dependent on the successful delivery of a current project?

<--- Score

227. Operational - will it work?

<--- Score

228. What trophy do we want on our mantle?

<--- Score

229. Who are you going to put out of business, and why?

<--- Score

230. What are the critical success factors?

<--- Score

231. How Will An ERP System Help My Business?

<--- Score

232. What am I trying to prove to myself, and how might it be hijacking my life and business success?

<--- Score

233. Is open source erp systems better than closed ones for medium sized businesses?

<--- Score

234. What ERP Applications (major functional areas such as Finance, SCM, Work Management and such) are currently implemented?

<--- Score

235. How does SAP Business One integrate with other stakeholder initiatives?
<--- Score

236. Find a success story of ERP implementation. What factors contributed to the success of this implementation?
<--- Score

237. If an institution contracts with an entity or individual to provide financial aid staffing or management for the administration of its Title IV programs, is the individual or entity considered a third-party servicer?
<--- Score

238. What is a third-party servicer?
<--- Score

239. How is training managed for the ERP system?
<--- Score

240. What is a feasible sequencing of reform initiatives over time?
<--- Score

241. Which Implementation Factors are Critical for Successful ERP Implementation?
<--- Score

242. What are the usability implications of SAP Business One actions?
<--- Score

243. Who will provide the final approval of SAP Business One deliverables?
<--- Score

244. How will we build a 100-year startup?
<--- Score

245. In what ways are SAP Business One vendors and us interacting to ensure safe and effective use?
<--- Score

246. What are strategies for increasing support and reducing opposition?
<--- Score

247. What is the range of capabilities?
<--- Score

248. Am I failing differently each time?
<--- Score

249. What kind of company can benefit from an erp system?
<--- Score

250. What is the best way to write a value proposition for a company offering erp systems?
<--- Score

251. Marketing budgets are tighter, consumers are more skeptical, and social media has changed forever the way we talk about SAP Business One. How do we gain traction?
<--- Score

252. What project outcomes of ERP projects can be included as dependent variables?

<--- Score

253. What are the Essentials of Internal SAP Business One Management?

<--- Score

254. What ERP software has B2B B2C eCommerce WebStore Integration?

<--- Score

255. What client groups is the system used with?

<--- Score

256. Do you have an implicit bias for capital investments over people investments?

<--- Score

257. Who is On the Team?

<--- Score

258. Where can we break convention?

<--- Score

259. Would you rather sell to knowledgeable and informed customers or to uninformed customers?

<--- Score

260. Do you see more potential in people than they do in themselves?

<--- Score

261. If you were responsible for initiating and implementing major changes in your organization, what steps might you take to ensure acceptance of

those changes?
<--- Score

262. Who are four people whose careers I've enhanced?
<--- Score

263. What is our SAP Business One Strategy?
<--- Score

264. Think of your SAP Business One project. what are the main functions?
<--- Score

265. Are we relevant? Will we be relevant five years from now? Ten?
<--- Score

266. Are you requiring the current organizational structure to be replicated in the new CPM/Cloud ERP system?
<--- Score

267. In retrospect, of the projects that we pulled the plug on, what percent do we wish had been allowed to keep going, and what percent do we wish had ended earlier?
<--- Score

268. How to get alignment between business strategy and IT infrastructure?
<--- Score

269. How can the use of ERP systems remove information or functional silos in your organization?

<--- Score

270. What are the business goals SAP Business One is aiming to achieve?
<--- Score

271. Is financial aid staffing or management considered a third-party service?
<--- Score

272. Are mobile devices being used and how many users are there?
<--- Score

273. How do critical success factors of ERP implementation change through the webbased business model cloud?
<--- Score

274. What are the implications of erp systems on the role of management accountants?
<--- Score

275. Who Uses SAP Business One?
<--- Score

276. Who is going to care?
<--- Score

277. Which criteria are used to determine which projects are going to be pursued or discarded?
<--- Score

278. What Are the Elements of an ERP System?
<--- Score

279. What are the success defining project outcomes in erp projects from the consulting parties perspective?
<--- Score

280. How to Secure SAP Business One?
<--- Score

281. What is Effective SAP Business One?
<--- Score

282. What constitutes an erp implementation failure?
<--- Score

283. What is Tricky About This?
<--- Score

284. What have we done to protect our business from competitive encroachment?
<--- Score

285. Are you requiring the current organizational structure to be replicated in a new cpm/cloud erp system?
<--- Score

286. What is the mission of the organization?
<--- Score

287. Design Thinking: Integrating Innovation, SAP Business One Experience, and Brand Value
<--- Score

288. What happens at this company when people fail?
<--- Score

289. What are the main reasons companies experience failures in implementing ERP systems?
<--- Score

290. How will we know if we have been successful?
<--- Score

291. Is there a moderating relation between distinctive characteristics of erp projects and the strength of the relation between methodology and erp project outcomes?
<--- Score

292. What may be the consequences for the performance of an organization if all stakeholders are not consulted regarding SAP Business One?
<--- Score

293. What is driving the ERP Movement?
<--- Score

294. What threat is SAP Business One addressing?
<--- Score

295. How will we insure seamless interoperability of SAP Business One moving forward?
<--- Score

296. Who is the interfacing system supplier?
<--- Score

297. How do we foster innovation?
<--- Score

298. What if a servicer instructs an institution not

to report it as a third-party servicer?
<--- Score

299. How do you compare ERP software?
<--- Score

300. Is there such a thing as choosing the right software or the right ERP software vendor?
<--- Score

301. What stupid rule would we most like to kill?
<--- Score

302. Which companies are working towards disrupting the ERP space that Oracle and SAP are in?
<--- Score

303. Where is our petri dish?
<--- Score

304. Your reputation and success is your lifeblood, and SAP Business One shows you how to stay relevant, add value, and win and retain customers
<--- Score

305. What are the best practices for integrating an e commerce site with a backend ERP or inventory management system?
<--- Score

306. What management system can we use to leverage the SAP Business One experience, ideas, and concerns of the people closest to the work to be done?
<--- Score

307. How does Cloud ERP handle custom code links?
<--- Score

308. To whom do you add value?
<--- Score

309. How important is SAP Business One to the user organizations mission?
<--- Score

310. Do we have enough freaky customers in our portfolio pushing us to the limit day in and day out?
<--- Score

311. How is the role of ERP system different from traditional TPS, MIS, DSS, and others?
<--- Score

312. What project outcomes of ERP projects can be derived from interviews?
<--- Score

313. What was the last experiment we ran?
<--- Score

314. Do SAP Business One rules make a reasonable demand on a users capabilities?
<--- Score

315. What is the craziest thing we can do?
<--- Score

316. Do I know what I'm doing? And who do I call if I don't?

<--- Score

317. Customization: out/in source, how willing?

<--- Score

318. What are the basics of SAP Business One fraud?

<--- Score

319. Are there any disadvantages to implementing SAP Business One? There might be some that are less obvious?

<--- Score

320. Do we think we know, or do we know we know ?

<--- Score

321. We picked a method, now what?

<--- Score

322. If I had to leave my organization for a year and the only communication I could have with employees was a single paragraph, what would I write?

<--- Score

323. When information truly is ubiquitous, when reach and connectivity are completely global, when computing resources are infinite, and when a whole new set of impossibilities are not only possible, but happening, what will that do to our business?

<--- Score

324. Are we / should we be Revolutionary or evolutionary?

<--- Score

325. An architecture -start with the CIF?
<--- Score

326. What is ERP offering?
<--- Score

327. How do we make it meaningful in connecting SAP Business One with what users do day-to-day?
<--- Score

328. What do we do when new problems arise?
<--- Score

329. How can we become more high-tech but still be high touch?
<--- Score

330. What does your signature ensure?
<--- Score

331. What are your most important goals for the strategic SAP Business One objectives?
<--- Score

332. Who have we, as a company, historically been when we've been at our best?
<--- Score

333. What is mySAP?
<--- Score

334. If every company in a sector is using the same so-called vanilla software (e.g. an SAP ERP system) what happens to the competitive advantage from implementing IT systems?

<--- Score

335. What Should You Be Worrying About ?
<--- Score

336. Consider what happens if the receiving application is migrated to a cloud service, and the ERP application remains in-house. What protocols do these applications use to talk to each other?
<--- Score

337. If you had to rebuild your organization without any traditional competitive advantages (i.e., no killer a technology, promising research, innovative product/service delivery model, etc.), how would your people have to approach their work and collaborate together in order to create the necessary conditions for success?
<--- Score

338. What will erp fix in my business?
<--- Score

339. In the past year, what have you done (or could you have done) to increase the accurate perception of this company/brand as ethical and honest?
<--- Score

340. What are the long-term SAP Business One goals?
<--- Score

341. Who Uses What?
<--- Score

342. How Does An ERP System Work?

<--- Score

343. Have benefits been optimized with all key stakeholders?
<--- Score

344. How would our PR, marketing, and social media change if we did not use outside agencies?
<--- Score

345. What are the main differences between the implementation of a WfMS and that of an ERP system?
<--- Score

346. How do we manage SAP Business One Knowledge Management (KM)?
<--- Score

Add up total points for this section:
_ _ _ _ _ = Total points for this section

Divided by: _ _ _ _ _ _ (number of statements answered) = _ _ _ _ _ _
Average score for this section

Transfer your score to the SAP Business One Index at the beginning of the Self-Assessment.

SAP Business One and Managing Projects, Criteria for Project Managers:

1.0 Initiating Process Group: SAP Business One

1. Establishment of pm office?

2. Where must it be done?

3. What are the tools and techniques to be used in each phase?

4. Measurable - are the targets measurable?

5. Were sponsors and decision makers available when needed outside regularly scheduled meetings?

6. Are you just doing busywork to pass the time?

7. Who supports, improves, and oversees standardized processes related to the SAP Business One projects program?

8. Do you understand the quality and control criteria that must be achieved for successful SAP Business One project completion?

9. During which stage of Risk planning are risks prioritized based on probability and impact?

10. If action is called for, what form should it take?

11. How well defined and documented were the SAP Business One project management processes you chose to use?

12. Who is involved in each phase?

13. Who is behind the SAP Business One project?

14. Who is funding the SAP Business One project?

15. What areas were overlooked on this SAP Business One project?

16. What business situation is being addressed?

17. At which stage, in a typical SAP Business One project do stake holders have maximum influence?

18. Do you know all the stakeholders impacted by the SAP Business One project and what needs are?

19. Who are the SAP Business One project stakeholders?

20. Did you use a contractor or vendor?

1.1 Project Charter: SAP Business One

21. What is in it for you?

22. How will you know a change is an improvement?

23. When do you use a SAP Business One project Charter?

24. Review the general mission What system will be affected by the improvement efforts?

25. Name and describe the elements that deal with providing the detail?

26. Will this replace an existing product?

27. When will this occur?

28. What barriers do you predict to your success?

29. What are you striving to accomplish (measurable goal(s))?

30. What does it need to do?

31. Who are the stakeholders?

32. Why the improvements?

33. What ideas do you have for initial tests of change (PDSA cycles)?

34. Why use a SAP Business One project charter?

35. Customer: who are you doing the SAP Business One project for?

36. What is the justification?

37. Assumptions: what factors, for planning purposes, are you considering to be true?

38. What are the constraints?

39. When?

40. Major high-level milestone targets: what events measure progress?

1.2 Stakeholder Register: SAP Business One

41. Is your organization ready for change?

42. How will reports be created?

43. How big is the gap?

44. Who is managing stakeholder engagement?

45. What are the major SAP Business One project milestones requiring communications or providing communications opportunities?

46. How should employers make voices heard?

47. How much influence do they have on the SAP Business One project?

48. What is the power of the stakeholder?

49. Who wants to talk about Security?

50. What & Why?

51. What opportunities exist to provide communications?

1.3 Stakeholder Analysis Matrix: SAP Business One

52. Own known vulnerabilities?

53. Vital contracts and partners?

54. Which conditions out of the control of the management are crucial for the achievement of the outputs?

55. Who will promote/support the SAP Business One project, provided that they are involved?

56. Does the stakeholder want to be involved or merely need to be informed about the SAP Business One project and its process?

57. If you can not fix it, how do you do it differently?

58. What do people from other organizations see as your organizations weaknesses?

59. Beneficiaries; who are the potential beneficiaries?

60. Effects on core activities, distraction?

61. It developments?

62. How can you counter negative efforts?

63. Will the impacts be local, national or international?

64. Do any safeguard policies apply to the SAP Business One project?

65. Marketing - reach, distribution, awareness?

66. What is the relationship among stakeholders?

67. What is your Risk Management?

68. Who will obstruct/hinder the SAP Business One project if they are not involved?

69. Disadvantages of proposition?

70. How to measure the achievement of the Development Objective?

2.0 Planning Process Group: SAP Business One

71. What do you need to do?

72. What is involved in SAP Business One project scope management, and why is good SAP Business One project scope management so important on information technology SAP Business One projects?

73. To what extent are the visions and actions of the partners consistent or divergent with regard to the program?

74. To what extent has the intervention strategy been adapted to the areas of intervention in which it is being implemented?

75. If you are late, will anybody notice?

76. How will users learn how to use the deliverables?

77. How are it SAP Business One projects different?

78. Have operating capacities been created and/or reinforced in partners?

79. When developing the estimates for SAP Business One project phases, you choose to add the individual estimates for the activities that comprise each phase. What type of estimation method are you using?

80. What do they need to know about the SAP

Business One project?

81. What is a Software Development Life Cycle (SDLC)?

82. You are creating your WBS and find that you keep decomposing tasks into smaller and smaller units. How can you tell when you are done?

83. How can you make your needs known?

84. How does activity resource estimation affect activity duration estimation?

85. What type of estimation method are you using?

86. How well defined and documented are the SAP Business One project management processes you chose to use?

87. Is the duration of the program sufficient to ensure a cycle that will SAP Business One project the sustainability of the interventions?

88. How should needs be met?

89. To what extent has a PMO contributed to raising the quality of the design of the SAP Business One project?

90. How many days can task X be late in starting without affecting the SAP Business One project completion date?

2.1 Project Management Plan: SAP Business One

91. Will you add a schedule and diagram?

92. What if, for example, the positive direction and vision of your organization causes expected trends to change resulting in greater need than expected?

93. What is SAP Business One project scope management?

94. Do the proposed changes from the SAP Business One project include any significant risks to safety?

95. What are the training needs?

96. Is there anything you would now do differently on your SAP Business One project based on past experience?

97. Are there any client staffing expectations?

98. Is mitigation authorized or recommended?

99. What should you drop in order to add something new?

100. If the SAP Business One project is complex or scope is specialized, do you have appropriate and/or qualified staff available to perform the tasks?

101. Are the proposed SAP Business One project

purposes different than a previously authorized SAP Business One project?

102. When is the SAP Business One project management plan created?

103. Who is the sponsor?

104. Is the engineering content at a feasibility level-of-detail, and is it sufficiently complete, to provide an adequate basis for the baseline cost estimate?

105. Has the selected plan been formulated using cost effectiveness and incremental analysis techniques?

106. Are there any scope changes proposed for a previously authorized SAP Business One project?

107. What is risk management?

108. What would you do differently what did not work?

2.2 Scope Management Plan: SAP Business One

109. What happens to rejected deliverables?

110. Materials available for performing the work?

111. Are agendas created for each meeting with meeting objectives, meeting topics, invitee list, and action items from past meetings?

112. Have external dependencies been captured in the schedule?

113. Pop quiz – which are the same inputs as in scope planning?

114. For which criterion is it tolerable not to meet the original parameters?

115. How do you know how you are doing?

116. Where do scope management processes fit in?

117. Is there an onboarding process in place?

118. Do you secure formal approval of changes and requirements from stakeholders?

119. Are there any windfall benefits that would accrue to the SAP Business One project sponsor or other parties?

120. When is corrective or preventative action required?

121. Has your organization done similar tasks before?

122. Personnel with expertise?

123. Has a capability assessment been conducted?

124. Are decisions captured in a decisions log?

125. Will your organizations estimating methodology be used and followed?

126. Are milestone deliverables effectively tracked and compared to SAP Business One project plan?

127. Assess the expected stability of the scope of this SAP Business One project how likely is it to change, how frequently, and by how much?

2.3 Requirements Management Plan: SAP Business One

128. How will the information be distributed?

129. Who is responsible for monitoring and tracking the SAP Business One project requirements?

130. After the requirements are gathered and set forth on the requirements register, theyre little more than a laundry list of items. Some may be duplicates, some might conflict with others and some will be too broad or too vague to understand. Describe how the requirements will be analyzed. Who will perform the analysis?

131. Is there formal agreement on who has authority to approve a change in requirements?

132. Will the product release be stable and mature enough to be deployed in the user community?

133. Is stakeholder risk tolerance an important factor for the requirements process in this SAP Business One project?

134. Is the user satisfied?

135. Is there formal agreement on who has authority to request a change in requirements?

136. Do you expect stakeholders to be cooperative?

137. In case of software development; Should you have a test for each code module?

138. What performance metrics will be used?

139. What are you trying to do?

140. What is a problem?

141. Are actual resource expenditures versus planned still acceptable?

142. Is the system software (non-operating system) new to the IT SAP Business One project team?

143. Did you distinguish the scope of work the contractor(s) will be required to do?

144. Which hardware or software, related to, or as outcome of the SAP Business One project is new to your organization?

145. Is requirements work dependent on any other specific SAP Business One project or non-SAP Business One project activities (e.g. funding, approvals, procurement)?

146. Is it new or replacing an existing business system or process?

147. Have stakeholders been instructed in the Change Control process?

2.4 Requirements Documentation: SAP Business One

148. Does the system provide the functions which best support the customers needs?

149. Validity. does the system provide the functions which best support the customers needs?

150. What is effective documentation?

151. What are current process problems?

152. Who provides requirements?

153. Basic work/business process; high-level, what is being touched?

154. How much testing do you need to do to prove that your system is safe?

155. What marketing channels do you want to use: e-mail, letter or sms?

156. What is a show stopper in the requirements?

157. Do technical resources exist?

158. Has requirements gathering uncovered information that would necessitate changes?

159. How does what is being described meet the business need?

160. Do your constraints stand?

161. How linear / iterative is your Requirements Gathering process (or will it be)?

162. How will they be documented / shared?

163. How can you document system requirements?

164. Who is interacting with the system?

165. How do you know when a Requirement is accurate enough?

166. Verifiability. can the requirements be checked?

167. What are the attributes of a customer?

2.5 Requirements Traceability Matrix: SAP Business One

168. How small is small enough?

169. How will it affect the stakeholders personally in their career?

170. How do you manage scope?

171. Will you use a Requirements Traceability Matrix?

172. What are the chronologies, contingencies, consequences, criteria?

173. Why do you manage scope?

174. Is there a requirements traceability process in place?

175. Describe the process for approving requirements so they can be added to the traceability matrix and SAP Business One project work can be performed. Will the SAP Business One project requirements become approved in writing?

176. What percentage of SAP Business One projects are producing traceability matrices between requirements and other work products?

177. Do you have a clear understanding of all subcontracts in place?

178. What is the WBS?

179. Why use a WBS?

2.6 Project Scope Statement: SAP Business One

180. Will you need a statement of work?

181. How often do you estimate that the scope might change, and why?

182. Elements that deal with providing the detail?

183. Will all tasks resulting from issues be entered into the SAP Business One project Plan and tracked through the plan?

184. Elements of scope management that deal with concept development ?

185. Once its defined, what is the stability of the SAP Business One project scope?

186. Is there a Quality Assurance Plan documented and filed?

187. What went wrong?

188. Is there an information system for the SAP Business One project?

189. If the scope changes, what will the impact be to your SAP Business One project in terms of duration, cost, quality, or any other important areas of the SAP Business One project?

190. What are the major deliverables of the SAP Business One project?

191. Change management vs. change leadership - what is the difference?

192. Is the SAP Business One project organization documented and on file?

193. Will there be a Change Control Process in place?

194. What is the product of this SAP Business One project?

195. What is the most common tool for helping define the detail?

196. Relevant - ask yourself can you get there; why are you doing this SAP Business One project?

197. Does the scope statement still need some clarity?

198. Were key SAP Business One project stakeholders brought into the SAP Business One project Plan?

2.7 Assumption and Constraint Log: SAP Business One

199. Are best practices and metrics employed to identify issues, progress, performance, etc.?

200. Has a SAP Business One project Communications Plan been developed?

201. Are there processes defining how software will be developed including development methods, overall timeline for development, software product standards, and traceability?

202. Can the requirements be traced to the appropriate components of the solution, as well as test scripts?

203. Are there procedures in place to effectively manage interdependencies with other SAP Business One projects / systems?

204. What other teams / processes would be impacted by changes to the current process, and how?

205. Is the amount of effort justified by the anticipated value of forming a new process?

206. When can log be discarded?

207. Have all necessary approvals been obtained?

208. Contradictory information between document

sections?

209. Does the system design reflect the requirements?

210. Is this process still needed?

211. Is this model reasonable?

212. Are you meeting your customers expectations consistently?

213. Does the document/deliverable meet general requirements (for example, statement of work) for all deliverables?

214. Would known impacts serve as impediments?

215. How can you prevent/fix violations?

216. What does an audit system look like?

217. Was the document/deliverable developed per the appropriate or required standards (for example, Institute of Electrical and Electronics Engineers standards)?

218. How relevant is this attribute to this SAP Business One project or audit?

2.8 Work Breakdown Structure: SAP Business One

219. Is it still viable?

220. Who has to do it?

221. How far down?

222. What has to be done?

223. Why is it useful?

224. When would you develop a Work Breakdown Structure?

225. Where does it take place?

226. When do you stop?

227. What is the probability of completing the SAP Business One project in less that xx days?

228. What is the probability that the SAP Business One project duration will exceed xx weeks?

229. Is the work breakdown structure (wbs) defined and is the scope of the SAP Business One project clear with assigned deliverable owners?

230. How much detail?

231. Do you need another level?

232. Why would you develop a Work Breakdown Structure?

233. Can you make it?

234. How will you and your SAP Business One project team define the SAP Business One projects scope and work breakdown structure?

235. Is it a change in scope?

236. How many levels?

237. When does it have to be done?

238. How big is a work-package?

2.9 WBS Dictionary: SAP Business One

239. Are retroactive changes to budgets for completed work specifically prohibited in an established procedure, and is this procedure adhered to?

240. The anticipated business volume?

241. Is budgeted cost for work performed calculated in a manner consistent with the way work is planned?

242. How detailed should a SAP Business One project get?

243. Are material costs reported within the same period as that in which BCWP is earned for that material?

244. Are internal budgets for authorized, and not priced changes based on the contractors resource plan for accomplishing the work?

245. Does the contractors system include procedures for measuring the performance of critical subcontractors?

246. Are records maintained to show full accountability for all material purchased for the contract, including the residual inventory?

247. Actual cost of work performed?

248. Are current budgets resulting from changes

to the authorized work and/or internal replanning, reconcilable to original budgets for specified reporting items?

249. Are retroactive changes to BCWS and BCWP prohibited except for correction of errors or for normal accounting adjustments?

250. Are estimates of costs at completion generated in a rational, consistent manner?

251. Are the requirements for all items of overhead established by rational, traceable processes?

252. The wbs is developed as part of a joint planning session. and how do you know that youhave done this right?

253. Performance to date and material commitment?

254. Are the contractors estimates of costs at completion reconcilable with cost data reported to us?

255. Are retroactive changes to direct costs and indirect costs prohibited except for the correction of errors and routine accounting adjustments?

256. What is the end result of a work package?

257. Budgets assigned to control accounts?

2.10 Schedule Management Plan: SAP Business One

258. Are SAP Business One project team members involved in detailed estimating and scheduling?

259. Is there an excessive and invalid use of task constraints and relationships of leads/lags?

260. Was the scope definition used in task sequencing?

261. Does the business case include how the SAP Business One project aligns with your organizations strategic goals & objectives?

262. Is a process defined for baseline approval and control?

263. Has process improvement efforts been completed before requirements efforts begin?

264. Is there an on-going process in place to monitor SAP Business One project risks?

265. Are metrics used to evaluate and manage Vendors?

266. Have the key elements of a coherent SAP Business One project management strategy been established?

267. Why conduct schedule analysis?

268. How are SAP Business One projects different from operations?

269. Are adequate resources provided for the quality assurance function?

270. Does the SAP Business One project have a formal SAP Business One project Charter?

271. Are scheduled deliverables actually delivered?

272. Is there an approved case?

273. Can be realistically shortened (the duration of subsequent tasks)?

274. Is a pmo (SAP Business One project management office) in place and provide oversight to the SAP Business One project?

275. Are all vendor contracts closed out?

2.11 Activity List: SAP Business One

276. How can the SAP Business One project be displayed graphically to better visualize the activities?

277. How should ongoing costs be monitored to try to keep the SAP Business One project within budget?

278. What is your organizations history in doing similar activities?

279. How detailed should a SAP Business One project get?

280. What is the probability the SAP Business One project can be completed in xx weeks?

281. When will the work be performed?

282. What is the total time required to complete the SAP Business One project if no delays occur?

283. Should you include sub-activities?

284. How difficult will it be to do specific activities on this SAP Business One project?

285. How will it be performed?

286. What went right?

287. When do the individual activities need to start and finish?

288. How do you determine the late start (LS) for each activity?

289. What did not go as well?

290. Where will it be performed?

291. How much slack is available in the SAP Business One project?

292. Are the required resources available or need to be acquired?

293. Is there anything planned that does not need to be here?

294. For other activities, how much delay can be tolerated?

2.12 Activity Attributes: SAP Business One

295. Were there other ways you could have organized the data to achieve similar results?

296. What conclusions/generalizations can you draw from this?

297. How many resources do you need to complete the work scope within a limit of X number of days?

298. Would you consider either of corresponding activities an outlier?

299. Activity: what is In the Bag?

300. Which method produces the more accurate cost assignment?

301. Is there a trend during the year?

302. Activity: fair or not fair?

303. Has management defined a definite timeframe for the turnaround or SAP Business One project window?

304. How many days do you need to complete the work scope with a limit of X number of resources?

305. Activity: what is Missing?

306. What is the general pattern here?

307. Can more resources be added?

308. Do you feel very comfortable with your prediction?

309. Resource is assigned to?

2.13 Milestone List: SAP Business One

310. Sustaining internal capabilities?

311. Loss of key staff?

312. It is to be a narrative text providing the crucial aspects of your SAP Business One project proposal answering what, who, how, when and where?

313. How will you get the word out to customers?

314. Identify critical paths (one or more) and which activities are on the critical path?

315. Usps (unique selling points)?

316. Competitive advantages?

317. How soon can the activity finish?

318. Timescales, deadlines and pressures?

319. Who will manage the SAP Business One project on a day-to-day basis?

320. What specific improvements did you make to the SAP Business One project proposal since the previous time?

321. When will the SAP Business One project be complete?

322. How late can each activity be finished and

started?

323. Reliability of data, plan predictability?

324. Insurmountable weaknesses?

325. Do you foresee any technical risks or developmental challenges?

326. Political effects?

327. What background experience, skills, and strengths does the team bring to your organization?

2.14 Network Diagram: SAP Business One

328. Can you calculate the confidence level?

329. What job or jobs follow it?

330. How difficult will it be to do specific activities on this SAP Business One project?

331. What to do and When?

332. If a current contract exists, can you provide the vendor name, contract start, and contract expiration date?

333. How confident can you be in your milestone dates and the delivery date?

334. What are the Major Administrative Issues?

335. Review the logical flow of the network diagram. Take a look at which activities you have first and then sequence the activities. Do they make sense?

336. What are the tools?

337. Exercise: what is the probability that the SAP Business One project duration will exceed xx weeks?

338. Planning: who, how long, what to do?

339. What activities must follow this activity?

340. Are the required resources available?

341. What job or jobs could run concurrently?

342. If x is long, what would be the completion time if you break x into two parallel parts of y weeks and z weeks?

343. What activity must be completed immediately before this activity can start?

344. What are the Key Success Factors?

345. Are you on time?

346. What is the lowest cost to complete this SAP Business One project in xx weeks?

2.15 Activity Resource Requirements: SAP Business One

347. Do you use tools like decomposition and rolling-wave planning to produce the activity list and other outputs?

348. Anything else?

349. Are there unresolved issues that need to be addressed?

350. Which logical relationship does the PDM use most often?

351. Time for overtime?

352. How do you handle petty cash?

353. How many signatures do you require on a check and does this match what is in your policy and procedures?

354. Why do you do that?

355. How do you manage time?

356. Organizational Applicability?

357. What are constraints that you might find during the Human Resource Planning process?

358. What is the Work Plan Standard?

359. When does monitoring begin?

360. Other support in specific areas?

2.16 Resource Breakdown Structure: SAP Business One

361. What can you do to improve productivity?

362. What defines a successful SAP Business One project?

363. Is predictive resource analysis being done?

364. Who delivers the information?

365. What is the difference between % Complete and % work?

366. Why do you do it?

367. Which resource planning tool provides information on resource responsibility and accountability?

368. The list could probably go on, but, the thing that you would most like to know is, How long & How much?

369. What is SAP Business One project communication management?

370. How difficult will it be to do specific activities on this SAP Business One project?

371. Why time management?

372. What are the requirements for resource data?

373. What is the primary purpose of the human resource plan?

374. Who needs what information?

375. Changes based on input from stakeholders?

376. When do they need the information?

377. Goals for the SAP Business One project. What is each stakeholders desired outcome for the SAP Business One project?

2.17 Activity Duration Estimates: SAP Business One

378. Is evaluation criteria defined to rate proposals?

379. Are contractor costs, schedule and technical performance monitored throughout the SAP Business One project?

380. How does SAP Business One project management relate to other disciplines?

381. What tasks must follow this task?

382. What type of activity sequencing method is required for corresponding activities?

383. Which is the BEST SAP Business One project management tool to use to determine the longest time the SAP Business One project will take?

384. Which is the BEST thing to do to try to complete a SAP Business One project two days earlier?

385. What is the duration of the critical path for this SAP Business One project?

386. What are the typical challenges SAP Business One project teams face during each of the five process groups?

387. Are risks that are likely to affect the SAP Business One project identified and documented?

388. SAP Business One project manager is using weighted average duration estimates to perform schedule network analysis. Which type of mathematical analysis is being used?

389. Could it have been avoided?

390. Are tools and techniques defined for gathering, integrating and distributing SAP Business One project outputs?

391. Research risk management software. Are many products available?

392. Does a process exist to determine the potential loss or gain if risk events occur?

393. How does the job market and current state of the economy affect human resource management?

394. Which includes asking team members about the time estimates for activities and reaching agreement on the calendar date for each activity?

395. What are crucial elements of successful SAP Business One project plan execution?

396. What are the main types of goods and services being outsourced?

2.18 Duration Estimating Worksheet: SAP Business One

397. Value pocket identification & quantification what are value pockets?

398. Science = process: remember the scientific method?

399. Is this operation cost effective?

400. Can the SAP Business One project be constructed as planned?

401. Why estimate costs?

402. When, then?

403. What info is needed?

404. How should ongoing costs be monitored to try to keep the SAP Business One project within budget?

405. Does the SAP Business One project provide innovative ways for stakeholders to overcome obstacles or deliver better outcomes?

406. When does your organization expect to be able to complete it?

407. How can the SAP Business One project be displayed graphically to better visualize the activities?

408. Is a construction detail attached (to aid in explanation)?

409. What is cost and SAP Business One project cost management?

410. Do any colleagues have experience with your organization and/or RFPs?

411. Define the work as completely as possible. What work will be included in the SAP Business One project?

412. What work will be included in the SAP Business One project?

413. What is next?

414. Is the SAP Business One project responsive to community need?

2.19 Project Schedule: SAP Business One

415. Master SAP Business One project schedule?

416. How can slack be negative?

417. What is the purpose of a SAP Business One project schedule?

418. Verify that the update is accurate. Are all remaining durations correct?

419. Should you have a test for each code module?

420. Are all remaining durations correct?

421. Why is software SAP Business One project disaster so common?

422. Did the final product meet or exceed user expectations?

423. Activity charts and bar charts are graphical representations of a SAP Business One project schedule ...how do they differ?

424. Your SAP Business One project management plan results in a SAP Business One project schedule that is too long. If the SAP Business One project network diagram cannot change and you have extra personnel resources, what is the BEST thing to do?

425. Did the SAP Business One project come in on schedule?

426. Is infrastructure setup part of your SAP Business One project?

427. Eliminate unnecessary activities. Are there activities that came from a template or previous SAP Business One project that are not applicable on this phase of this SAP Business One project?

428. What is the difference?

429. Are the original SAP Business One project schedule and budget realistic?

430. What documents, if any, will the subcontractor provide (eg SAP Business One project schedule, quality plan etc)?

431. Why or why not?

432. How effectively were issues able to be resolved without impacting the SAP Business One project Schedule or Budget?

2.20 Cost Management Plan: SAP Business One

433. Are the payment terms being followed?

434. What is an Acceptance Management Process?

435. Outside experts?

436. Resources – how will human resources be scheduled during each phase of the SAP Business One project?

437. Have all unresolved risks been documented?

438. Is the steering committee active in SAP Business One project oversight?

439. Cost estimate preparation – What cost estimates will be prepared during the SAP Business One project phases?

440. Are estimating assumptions and constraints captured?

441. Is stakeholder involvement adequate?

442. Change types and category – What are the types of changes and what are the techniques to report and control changes?

443. Is the SAP Business One project sponsor clearly communicating the business case or rationale for why

this SAP Business One project is needed?

444. Is the assigned SAP Business One project manager a PMP (Certified SAP Business One project manager) and experienced?

445. Are written status reports provided on a designated frequent basis?

446. What will be the split of responsibilities of progress measurement and controls among the owner, contractor, subcontractors, and vendors?

447. Are there checklists created to determine if all quality processes are followed?

448. Has your organization readiness assessment been conducted?

449. Risk Analysis?

450. Are quality inspections and review activities listed in the SAP Business One project schedule(s)?

451. Do SAP Business One project managers participating in the SAP Business One project know the SAP Business One projects true status first hand?

452. Are corrective actions and variances reported?

2.21 Activity Cost Estimates: SAP Business One

453. The impact and what actions were taken?

454. What is a SAP Business One project Management Plan?

455. How Award?

456. What communication items need improvement?

457. What is included in indirect cost being allocated?

458. What defines a successful SAP Business One project?

459. How do you change activities?

460. Is there anything unique in this SAP Business One projects scope statement that will affect resources?

461. What areas were overlooked on this SAP Business One project?

462. Is costing method consistent with study goals?

463. Who determines when the contractor is paid?

464. What is the estimators estimating history?

465. How quickly can the task be done with the skills available?

466. Were the costs or charges reasonable?

467. Who & what determines the need for contracted services?

468. Certification of actual expenditures?

469. What makes a good expected result statement?

470. Review – what are some common errors in activities to avoid?

471. Can you delete activities or make them inactive?

472. What is the activity inventory?

2.22 Cost Estimating Worksheet: SAP Business One

473. What happens to any remaining funds not used?

474. Ask: are others positioned to know, are others credible, and will others cooperate?

475. Identify the timeframe necessary to monitor progress and collect data to determine how the selected measure has changed?

476. Is the SAP Business One project responsive to community need?

477. Is it feasible to establish a control group arrangement?

478. Can a trend be established from historical performance data on the selected measure and are the criteria for using trend analysis or forecasting methods met?

479. What will others want?

480. What additional SAP Business One project(s) could be initiated as a result of this SAP Business One project?

481. Does the SAP Business One project provide innovative ways for stakeholders to overcome obstacles or deliver better outcomes?

482. What costs are to be estimated?

483. Will the SAP Business One project collaborate with the local community and leverage resources?

484. What is the estimated labor cost today based upon this information?

485. What can be included?

486. What is the purpose of estimating?

487. Who is best positioned to know and assist in identifying corresponding factors?

488. How will the results be shared and to whom?

2.23 Cost Baseline: SAP Business One

489. If you sold 10x widgets on a day, what would the affect on profits be?

490. How likely is it to go wrong?

491. What does a good WBS NOT look like?

492. Has operations management formally accepted responsibility for operating and maintaining the product(s) or service(s) delivered by the SAP Business One project?

493. Has the SAP Business One project documentation been archived or otherwise disposed as described in the SAP Business One project communication plan?

494. Is there anything you need from upper management in order to be successful?

495. Does a process exist for establishing a cost baseline to measure SAP Business One project performance?

496. What is your organizations history in doing similar tasks?

497. Should a more thorough impact analysis be conducted?

498. Has the SAP Business One project (or SAP Business One project phase) been evaluated against each objective established in the product description

and Integrated SAP Business One project Plan?

499. Have the resources used by the SAP Business One project been reassigned to other units or SAP Business One projects?

500. SAP Business One project goals -should others be reconsidered?

501. Are there contingencies or conditions related to the acceptance?

502. Does the suggested change request represent a desired enhancement to the products functionality?

503. Escalation criteria met?

504. Vac -variance at completion, how much over/ under budget do you expect to be?

505. What can go wrong?

506. How long are you willing to wait before you find out were late?

507. What do you want to measure ?

2.24 Quality Management Plan: SAP Business One

508. Show/provide copy of procedures for taking field notes?

509. What key performance indicators does your organization use to measure, manage, and improve key processes?

510. Is there a Steering Committee in place?

511. How are records kept in the office?

512. What is the Quality Management Plan?

513. How are people conducting sampling trained?

514. How are new requirements or changes to requirements identified?

515. How do senior leaders review organizational performance?

516. How are changes recorded?

517. How do you field-modify testing procedures?

518. How effectively was the Quality Management Plan applied during SAP Business One project Execution?

519. How relevant is this attribute to this SAP Business

One project or audit?

520. Does the program use modeling in the permitting or decision-making processes?

521. Sampling part of task?

522. How are changes approved?

523. How is equipment calibrated?

524. Have you eliminated all duplicative tasks or manual efforts, where appropriate?

525. Were there any deficiencies / issues in prior years self-assessment?

526. Have SAP Business One project management standards and procedures been established and documented?

527. Was trending evident between audits?

2.25 Quality Metrics: SAP Business One

528. What about still open problems?

529. What method of measurement do you use?

530. How does one achieve stability?

531. Is the reporting frequency appropriate?

532. How do you know if everyone is trying to improve the right things?

533. Should a modifier be included?

534. Did evaluation start on time?

535. How effective are your security tests?

536. What if the biggest risk to your business were the already stated people who do not complain?

537. What happens if you get an abnormal result?

538. Are applicable standards referenced and available?

539. How exactly do you define when differences exist?

540. What is the timeline to meet your goal?

541. Which report did you use to create the data you are submitting?

542. How do you measure?

543. Are quality metrics defined?

544. Were quality attributes reported?

545. How can the effectiveness of each of the activities be measured?

546. Have risk areas been identified?

547. Was the overall quality better or worse than previous products?

2.26 Process Improvement Plan: SAP Business One

548. What lessons have you learned so far?

549. Have the supporting tools been developed or acquired?

550. Are you following the quality standards?

551. How do you manage quality?

552. Does explicit definition of the measures exist?

553. What personnel are the sponsors for that initiative?

554. Are you meeting the quality standards?

555. Where do you want to be?

556. What is the test-cycle concept?

557. Where are you now?

558. What is quality and how will you ensure it?

559. If a process improvement framework is being used, which elements will help the problems and goals listed?

560. What actions are needed to address the problems and achieve the goals?

561. The motive is determined by asking, Why do you want to achieve this goal?

562. Have the frequency of collection and the points in the process where measurements will be made been determined?

563. Has a process guide to collect the data been developed?

564. Where do you focus?

565. Purpose of goal: the motive is determined by asking, why do you want to achieve this goal?

566. Everyone agrees on what process improvement is, right?

567. Are there forms and procedures to collect and record the data?

2.27 Responsibility Assignment Matrix: SAP Business One

568. Changes in the direct base to which overhead costs are allocated?

569. Major functional areas of contract effort?

570. The total budget for the contract (including estimates for authorized and unpriced work)?

571. Are records maintained to show how management reserves are used?

572. What simple tool can you use to help identify and prioritize SAP Business One project risks that is very low tech and high touch?

573. Cwbs elements to be subcontracted, with identification of subcontractors?

574. Do work packages consist of discrete tasks which are adequately described?

575. Does the accounting system provide a basis for auditing records of direct costs chargeable to the contract?

576. Are the bases and rates for allocating costs from each indirect pool consistently applied?

577. Most people let you know when others re too busy, and are others really too busy?

578. What cost control tool do many experts say is crucial to SAP Business One project management?

579. What are the assigned resources?

580. Is cost and schedule performance measurement done in a consistent, systematic manner?

581. Are indirect costs accumulated for comparison with the corresponding budgets?

582. Who is going to do that work?

583. Availability – will the group or the person be available within the necessary time interval?

584. What expertise is available in your department?

585. Does a missing responsibility indicate that the current SAP Business One project is not yet fully understood?

2.28 Roles and Responsibilities: SAP Business One

586. What is working well?

587. Are the quality assurance functions and related roles and responsibilities clearly defined?

588. Is the data complete?

589. Influence: what areas of organizational decision making are you able to influence when you do not have authority to make the final decision?

590. What areas of supervision are challenging for you?

591. Is there a training program in place for stakeholders covering expectations, roles and responsibilities and any addition knowledge others need to be good stakeholders?

592. Are governance roles and responsibilities documented?

593. Key conclusions and recommendations: Are conclusions and recommendations relevant and acceptable?

594. Are SAP Business One project team roles and responsibilities identified and documented?

595. Was the expectation clearly communicated?

596. Be specific; avoid generalities. Thank you and great work alone are insufficient. What exactly do you appreciate and why?

597. What should you highlight for improvement?

598. Concern: where are you limited or have no authority, where you can not influence?

599. Who is involved?

600. Do you take the time to clearly define roles and responsibilities on SAP Business One project tasks?

601. Is feedback clearly communicated and non-judgmental?

602. What should you do now to prepare yourself for a promotion, increased responsibilities or a different job?

603. What is working well within your organizations performance management system?

604. What areas would you highlight for changes or improvements?

605. To decide whether to use a quality measurement, ask how will you know when it is achieved?

2.29 Human Resource Management Plan: SAP Business One

606. How to convince employees that this is a necessary process?

607. Was your organizations estimating methodology being used and followed?

608. Are software metrics formally captured, analyzed and used as a basis for other SAP Business One project estimates?

609. Are schedule deliverables actually delivered?

610. Have stakeholder accountabilities & responsibilities been clearly defined?

611. Has the business need been clearly defined?

612. Have the key elements of a coherent SAP Business One project management strategy been established?

613. Is SAP Business One project status reviewed with the steering and executive teams at appropriate intervals?

614. Was the SAP Business One project schedule reviewed by all stakeholders and formally accepted?

615. Has the budget been baselined?

616. Does all SAP Business One project documentation reside in a common repository for easy access?

617. Has a structured approach been used to break work effort into manageable components (WBS)?

618. Is the SAP Business One project schedule available for all SAP Business One project team members to review?

619. Are the people assigned to the SAP Business One project sufficiently qualified?

620. Does the SAP Business One project have a formal SAP Business One project Charter?

621. Are status reports received per the SAP Business One project Plan?

622. Is the communication plan being followed?

2.30 Communications Management Plan: SAP Business One

623. Do you have members of your team responsible for certain stakeholders?

624. Do you then often overlook a key stakeholder or stakeholder group?

625. Which stakeholders can influence others?

626. Who will use or be affected by the result of a SAP Business One project?

627. What does the stakeholder need from the team?

628. Is there an important stakeholder who is actively opposed and will not receive messages?

629. Do you ask; can you recommend others for you to talk with about this initiative?

630. What is the political influence?

631. What are the interrelationships?

632. Can you think of other people who might have concerns or interests?

633. Are you constantly rushing from meeting to meeting?

634. Do you feel a register helps?

635. Timing: when do the effects of the communication take place?

636. Why manage stakeholders?

637. Who to learn from?

638. Where do team members get information?

639. What communications method?

640. Is the stakeholder role recognized by your organization?

641. Why do you manage communications?

642. Who are the members of the governing body?

2.31 Risk Management Plan: SAP Business One

643. Are the required plans included, such as nonstructural flood risk management plans?

644. How much risk can you tolerate?

645. Monitoring -what factors can you track that will enable you to determine if the risk is becoming more or less likely?

646. Is the customer willing to commit significant time to the requirements gathering process?

647. Why might it be late?

648. Are the software tools integrated with each other?

649. Does the SAP Business One project have the authority and ability to avoid the risk?

650. Are status updates being made on schedule and are the updates clearly described?

651. Maximize short-term return on investment?

652. People risk -are people with appropriate skills available to help complete the SAP Business One project?

653. What risks are tracked?

654. Are tool mentors available?

655. Is there anything you would now do differently on your SAP Business One project based on this experience?

656. Can the SAP Business One project proceed without assuming the risk?

657. Risk documentation: what reporting formats and processes will be used for risk management activities?

658. Why is product liability a serious issue?

659. What worked well?

660. Where do risks appear in the business phases?

661. What is the likelihood?

2.32 Risk Register: SAP Business One

662. Who is going to do it?

663. Preventative actions - planned actions to reduce the likelihood a risk will occur and/or reduce the seriousness should it occur. What should you do now?

664. Does the evidence highlight any areas to advance opportunities or foster good relations. If yes what steps will be taken?

665. Financial risk -can your organization afford to undertake the SAP Business One project?

666. Assume the event happens, what is the Most Likely impact?

667. Are your objectives at risk?

668. What are the main aims, objectives of the policy, strategy, or service and the intended outcomes?

669. User involvement: do you have the right users?

670. People risk -are people with appropriate skills available to help complete the SAP Business One project?

671. How are risks graded?

672. What is a Risk?

673. What may happen or not go according to plan?

674. What has changed since the last period?

675. What should the audit role be in establishing a risk management process?

676. What should you do when?

677. Methodology: how will risk management be performed on this SAP Business One project?

678. What are you going to do to limit the SAP Business One projects risk exposure due to the identified risks?

679. What are your key risks/show istoppers and what is being done to manage them?

680. What is the appropriate level of risk management for this SAP Business One project?

681. Cost/benefit – how much will the proposed mitigations cost and how does this cost compare with the potential cost of the risk event/situation should it occur?

2.33 Probability and Impact Assessment: SAP Business One

682. Is the number of people on the SAP Business One project team adequate to do the job?

683. Are there any SAP Business One projects similar to this one in existence?

684. Which of corresponding risk factors can be avoided altogether?

685. Assuming that you have identified a number of risks in the SAP Business One project, how would you prioritize them?

686. What is the likely future demand of the customer?

687. When and how will the recent breakthroughs in basic research lead to commercial products?

688. Are enough people available?

689. Who should be responsible for the monitoring and tracking of the indicators youhave identified?

690. Does the customer have a solid idea of what is required?

691. Why has this particular mode of contracting been chosen?

692. Are the best people available?

693. Mitigation -how can you avoid the risk?

694. Risk may be made during which step of risk management?

695. Will there be an increase in the political conservatism?

696. Would avoiding any of corresponding impact the SAP Business One projects chance of success?

697. Do you manage the process through use of metrics?

698. What is the experience (performance, attitude, business ethics, etc.) in the past with contractors?

699. How is risk handled within this SAP Business One project organization?

700. What are the preparations required for facing difficulties?

2.34 Probability and Impact Matrix: SAP Business One

701. How are you working with risks?

702. Which of your SAP Business One projects should be selected when compared with other SAP Business One projects?

703. How do risks change during the SAP Business One projects life cycle?

704. Lay ground work for future returns?

705. Non-valid or incredible information?

706. Do you have a consistent repeatable process that is actually used?

707. Have you worked with the customer in the past?

708. Which risks need to move on to Perform Quantitative Risk Analysis?

709. What are the chances the risk events will occur?

710. Are people attending meetings and doing work?

711. What should be done with risks on the watch list?

712. What should be done with non-critical risks?

713. Have top software and customer managers

formally committed to support the SAP Business One project?

714. What is the impact if the risk does occur?

715. What is the industrial relations prevailing in this organization?

716. Who has experience with this?

717. What action do you usually take against risks?

718. Are team members trained in the use of the tools?

719. What are data sources?

2.35 Risk Data Sheet: SAP Business One

720. Who has a vested interest in how you perform as your organization (our stakeholders)?

721. How can hazards be reduced?

722. What will be the consequences if it happens?

723. What if client refuses?

724. What are the main threats to your existence?

725. Potential for recurrence?

726. How do you handle product safely?

727. What do people affected think about the need for, and practicality of preventive measures?

728. Are new hazards created?

729. What is the duration of infection (the length of time the host is infected with the organizm) in a normal healthy human host?

730. What do you know?

731. What are you trying to achieve (Objectives)?

732. Is the data sufficiently specified in terms of the type of failure being analyzed, and its frequency or

probability?

733. Risk of what?

734. Type of risk identified?

735. What were the Causes that contributed?

736. Do effective diagnostic tests exist?

737. How can it happen?

738. What are the main opportunities available to you that you should grab while you can?

739. During work activities could hazards exist?

2.36 Procurement Management Plan: SAP Business One

740. Are the quality tools and methods identified in the Quality Plan appropriate to the SAP Business One project?

741. Are the results of quality assurance reviews provided to affected groups & individuals?

742. Were SAP Business One project team members involved in the development of activity & task decomposition?

743. Have lessons learned been conducted after each SAP Business One project release?

744. How long will it take for the purchase cost to be the same as the lease cost?

745. What areas are overlooked on this SAP Business One project?

746. Is there a formal set of procedures supporting Issues Management?

747. Have the key functions and capabilities been defined and assigned to each release or iteration?

748. Are meeting minutes captured and sent out after meetings?

749. Has a resource management plan been created?

750. Have reserves been created to address risks?

751. What were things that you did very well and want to do the same again on the next SAP Business One project?

752. Is there any form of automated support for Issues Management?

753. Are the appropriate IT resources adequate to meet planned commitments?

754. Has the SAP Business One project scope been baselined?

755. Are change requests logged and managed?

2.37 Source Selection Criteria: SAP Business One

756. Have team members been adequately trained?

757. How is past performance evaluated?

758. What should clarifications include?

759. What documentation should be used to support the selection decision?

760. What are the special considerations for preaward debriefings?

761. Can you make a cost/technical tradeoff?

762. In order of importance, which evaluation criteria are the most critical to the determination of your overall rating?

763. Do you have designated specific forms or worksheets?

764. What documentation is necessary regarding electronic communications?

765. What evidence should be provided regarding proposal evaluations?

766. Will the technical evaluation factor unnecessarily force the acquisition into a higher-priced market segment?

767. What management structure does your organization consider as optimal for performing the contract?

768. Is there collaboration among your evaluators?

769. What source selection software is your team using?

770. When should debriefings be held and how should they be scheduled?

771. How should the oral presentations be handled?

772. How are oral presentations documented?

773. Are resultant proposal revisions allowed?

774. What documentation is needed for a tradeoff decision?

775. What are the steps in performing a cost/tech tradeoff?

2.38 Stakeholder Management Plan: SAP Business One

776. Why would a customer be interested in a particular product or service?

777. Are the people assigned to the SAP Business One project sufficiently qualified?

778. Has a quality assurance plan been developed for the SAP Business One project?

779. Who will perform the review(s)?

780. How is information analyzed, and what specific pieces of data would be of interest to the SAP Business One project manager?

781. Who would sign off on the charter?

782. Are meeting minutes captured and sent out after the meeting?

783. How much information should be collected?

784. Are SAP Business One project team members involved in detailed estimating and scheduling?

785. What is the difference between product and SAP Business One project scope?

786. Is the assigned SAP Business One project manager a PMP (Certified SAP Business One project

manager) and experienced?

787. Does the SAP Business One project have a formal SAP Business One project Plan?

788. Has the schedule been baselined?

789. Is pert / critical path or equivalent methodology being used?

790. Are milestone deliverables effectively tracked and compared to SAP Business One project plan?

791. What potential impact does the stakeholder have on the SAP Business One project?

2.39 Change Management Plan: SAP Business One

792. How does the principle of senders and receivers make the SAP Business One project communications effort more complex?

793. Identify the current level of skills and knowledge and behaviours of the group that will be impacted on. What prerequisite knowledge do corresponding groups need?

794. What prerequisite knowledge do corresponding groups need?

795. Who will fund the training?

796. What skills, education, knowledge, or work experiences should the resources have for each identified competency?

797. What tasks are needed?

798. Will a different work structure focus people on what is important?

799. Has the relevant business unit been notified of installation and support requirements?

800. What processes are in place to manage knowledge about the SAP Business One project?

801. Who is responsible for which tasks?

802. What are the major changes to processes?

803. What is the worst thing that can happen if you chose not to communicate this information?

804. Has the training co-ordinator been provided with the training details and put in place the necessary arrangements?

805. Does this change represent a completely new process for your organization, or a different application of an existing process?

806. Has a training need analysis been carried out?

807. How can you best frame the message so that it addresses the audiences interests?

808. Identify the risk and assess the significance and likelihood of it occurring and plan the contingency What risks may occur upfront?

809. Is there an adequate supply of people for the new roles?

810. What communication network would you use – informal or formal?

3.0 Executing Process Group: SAP Business One

811. Does the SAP Business One project team have enough people to execute the SAP Business One project plan?

812. Who will be the main sponsor?

813. Could a new application negatively affect the current IT infrastructure?

814. What is the product of your SAP Business One project?

815. What are the critical steps involved in selecting measures and initiatives?

816. What are the challenges SAP Business One project teams face?

817. What type of people would you want on your team?

818. Is the program supported by national and/or local organizations?

819. What is the critical path for this SAP Business One project and how long is it?

820. If a risk event occurs, what will you do?

821. What areas does the group agree are the biggest

success on the SAP Business One project?

822. Is the SAP Business One project making progress in helping to achieve the set results?

823. What are crucial elements of successful SAP Business One project plan execution?

824. How many different communication channels does the SAP Business One project team have?

825. Mitigate. what will you do to minimize the impact should a risk event occur?

3.1 Team Member Status Report: SAP Business One

826. Does the product, good, or service already exist within your organization?

827. How will resource planning be done?

828. Are the products of your organizations SAP Business One projects meeting customers objectives?

829. Are the attitudes of staff regarding SAP Business One project work improving?

830. Does your organization have the means (staff, money, contract, etc.) to produce or to acquire the product, good, or service?

831. Is there evidence that staff is taking a more professional approach toward management of your organizations SAP Business One projects?

832. Will the staff do training or is that done by a third party?

833. How much risk is involved?

834. Do you have an Enterprise SAP Business One project Management Office (EPMO)?

835. When a teams productivity and success depend on collaboration and the efficient flow of information, what generally fails them?

836. How it is to be done?

837. What specific interest groups do you have in place?

838. Does every department have to have a SAP Business One project Manager on staff?

839. The problem with Reward & Recognition Programs is that the truly deserving people all too often get left out. How can you make it practical?

840. Why is it to be done?

841. How can you make it practical?

842. What is to be done?

843. How does this product, good, or service meet the needs of the SAP Business One project and your organization as a whole?

844. Are your organizations SAP Business One projects more successful over time?

3.2 Change Request: SAP Business One

845. What kind of information about the change request needs to be captured?

846. How does your organization control changes before and after software is released to a customer?

847. What must be taken into consideration when introducing change control programs?

848. Who is communicating the change?

849. How fast will change requests be approved?

850. Why do you want to have a change control system?

851. For which areas does this operating procedure apply?

852. What is the change request log?

853. How are changes requested (forms, method of communication)?

854. Will all change requests be unconditionally tracked through this process?

855. How shall the implementation of changes be recorded?

856. How is the change documented (format, content, storage)?

857. Customer acceptance plan how will the customer verify the change has been implemented successfully?

858. Have scm procedures for noting the change, recording it, and reporting it been followed?

859. Who is included in the change control team?

860. What is the purpose of change control?

861. Are there requirements attributes that are strongly related to the complexity and size?

862. What should be regulated in a change control operating instruction?

863. Who has responsibility for approving and ranking changes?

864. Why were your requested changes rejected or not made?

3.3 Change Log: SAP Business One

865. How does this relate to the standards developed for specific business processes?

866. Do the described changes impact on the integrity or security of the system?

867. Where do changes come from?

868. Is the change request open, closed or pending?

869. Is the change backward compatible without limitations?

870. Will the SAP Business One project fail if the change request is not executed?

871. Is the requested change request a result of changes in other SAP Business One project(s)?

872. When was the request approved?

873. Is this a mandatory replacement?

874. Is the submitted change a new change or a modification of a previously approved change?

875. When was the request submitted?

876. How does this change affect scope?

877. How does this change affect the timeline of the schedule?

878. Does the suggested change request seem to represent a necessary enhancement to the product?

879. Is the change request within SAP Business One project scope?

880. Who initiated the change request?

3.4 Decision Log: SAP Business One

881. What alternatives/risks were considered?

882. It becomes critical to track and periodically revisit both operational effectiveness; Are you noticing all that you need to, and are you interpreting what you see effectively?

883. Behaviors; what are guidelines that the team has identified that will assist them with getting the most out of team meetings?

884. How consolidated and comprehensive a story can you tell by capturing currently available incident data in a central location and through a log of key decisions during an incident?

885. Decision-making process; how will the team make decisions?

886. Does anything need to be adjusted?

887. Which variables make a critical difference?

888. Meeting purpose; why does this team meet?

889. Adversarial environment. is your opponent open to a non-traditional workflow, or will it likely challenge anything you do?

890. How does the use a Decision Support System influence the strategies/tactics or costs?

891. What is the average size of your matters in an applicable measurement?

892. Do strategies and tactics aimed at less than full control reduce the costs of management or simply shift the cost burden?

893. How do you define success?

894. What eDiscovery problem or issue did your organization set out to fix or make better?

895. What makes you different or better than others companies selling the same thing?

896. What is the line where eDiscovery ends and document review begins?

897. With whom was the decision shared or considered?

898. Linked to original objective?

899. What is your overall strategy for quality control / quality assurance procedures?

900. How effective is maintaining the log at facilitating organizational learning?

3.5 Quality Audit: SAP Business One

901. Are measuring and test equipment that have been placed out of service suitably identified and excluded from use in any device reconditioning operation?

902. How does your organization know that its staff are presenting original work, and properly acknowledging the work of others?

903. How does your organization know that its system for governing staff behaviour is appropriately effective and constructive?

904. How is the Strategic Plan (and other plans) reviewed and revised?

905. It is inappropriate to seek information about the Audit Panels preliminary views including questions like why do you ask that?

906. Are all employees made aware of device defects which may occur from the improper performance of specific jobs?

907. Statements of intent remain exactly that until they are put into effect. The next step is to deploy the already stated intentions. In other words, do the plans happen in reality?

908. Are all records associated with the reconditioning of a device maintained for a minimum of two years after the sale or disposal of the last device within a lot

of merchandise?

909. How does your organization know that its processes for managing severance are appropriately effective, constructive and fair?

910. How does your organization know that the range and quality of its accommodation, catering and transportation services are appropriately effective and constructive?

911. How does your organization know that its relationships with industry and employers are appropriately effective and constructive?

912. How does your organization know that its system for attending to the particular needs of its international staff is appropriately effective and constructive?

913. How does your organization know that its system for recruiting the best staff possible are appropriately effective and constructive?

914. How does your organization know that its promotions system is appropriately effective, constructive and fair?

915. How do you indicate the extent to which your personnel would be expected to contribute to the work effort?

916. How does your organization know that its planning processes are appropriately effective and constructive?

917. For each device to be reconditioned, are device specifications, such as appropriate engineering drawings, component specifications and software specifications, maintained?

918. Do the suppliers use a formal quality system?

919. What happens if your organization fails its Quality Audit?

3.6 Team Directory: SAP Business One

920. Decisions: what could be done better to improve the quality of the constructed product?

921. Who are your stakeholders (customers, sponsors, end users, team members)?

922. Who should receive information (all stakeholders)?

923. When does information need to be distributed?

924. Have you decided when to celebrate the SAP Business One projects completion date?

925. Process decisions: how well was task order work performed?

926. Process decisions: do job conditions warrant additional actions to collect job information and document on-site activity?

927. Does a SAP Business One project team directory list all resources assigned to the SAP Business One project?

928. How do unidentified risks impact the outcome of the SAP Business One project?

929. Is construction on schedule?

930. Decisions: is the most suitable form of contract being used?

931. How will the team handle changes?

932. What needs to be communicated?

933. Who will write the meeting minutes and distribute?

934. When will you produce deliverables?

935. Timing: when do the effects of communication take place?

936. How will you accomplish and manage the objectives?

937. Who are the Team Members?

3.7 Team Operating Agreement: SAP Business One

938. Did you draft the meeting agenda?

939. Do you send out the agenda and meeting materials in advance?

940. Does your team need access to all documents and information at all times?

941. How will you resolve conflict efficiently and respectfully?

942. Resource allocation: how will individual team members account for time and expenses, and how will this be allocated in the team budget?

943. What is group supervision?

944. Do you record meetings for the already stated unable to attend?

945. What are the boundaries (organizational or geographic) within which you operate?

946. What went well?

947. Why does your organization want to participate in teaming?

948. What resources can be provided for the team in terms of equipment, space, time for training,

protected time and space for meetings, and travel allowances?

949. Did you delegate tasks such as taking meeting minutes, presenting a topic and soliciting input?

950. What is a Virtual Team?

951. Do you prevent individuals from dominating the meeting?

952. What are some potential sources of conflict among team members?

953. Do you listen for voice tone and word choice to understand the meaning behind words?

954. Are there more than two national cultures represented by your team?

955. Are there differences in access to communication and collaboration technology based on team member location?

956. What is the anticipated procedure (recruitment, solicitation of volunteers, or assignment) for selecting team members?

957. Are there more than two functional areas represented by your team?

3.8 Team Performance Assessment: SAP Business One

958. To what degree can all members engage in open and interactive considerations?

959. Can familiarity breed backup?

960. To what degree does the teams purpose contain themes that are particularly meaningful and memorable?

961. To what degree does the teams approach to its work allow for modification and improvement over time?

962. Where to from here?

963. Do you give group members authority to make at least some important decisions?

964. To what degree do team members frequently explore the teams purpose and its implications?

965. When a reviewer complains about method variance, what is the essence of the complaint?

966. To what degree do team members feel that the purpose of the team is important, if not exciting?

967. Is there a particular method of data analysis that you would recommend as a means of demonstrating that method variance is not of great concern for a

given dataset?

968. To what degree are sub-teams possible or necessary?

969. Effects of crew composition on crew performance: Does the whole equal the sum of its parts?

970. What do you think is the most constructive thing that could be done now to resolve considerations and disputes about method variance?

971. To what degree are the teams goals and objectives clear, simple, and measurable?

972. To what degree are the skill areas critical to team performance present?

973. To what degree will team members, individually and collectively, commit time to help themselves and others learn and develop skills?

974. To what degree does the teams work approach provide opportunity for members to engage in results-based evaluation?

975. Do you promptly inform members about major developments that may affect them?

976. How does SAP Business One project termination impact SAP Business One project team members?

977. To what degree are the goals realistic?

3.9 Team Member Performance Assessment: SAP Business One

978. How do you start collaborating?

979. What stakeholders must be involved in the development and oversight of the performance plan?

980. What are the key duties or tasks of the Ratee?

981. To what degree are the relative importance and priority of the goals clear to all team members?

982. Are any validation activities performed?

983. What instructional strategies were developed/incorporated (e.g., direct instruction, indirect instruction, experiential learning, independent study, interactive instruction)?

984. What are the standards or expectations for success?

985. What specific plans do you have for developing effective cross-platform assessments in a blended learning environment?

986. Which training platform formats (i.e., mobile, virtual, videogame-based) were implemented in your effort(s)?

987. Is there reluctance to join a team?

988. How do you make use of research?

989. Does statute or regulation require the job responsibility?

990. What happens if a team member disagrees with the Job Expectations?

991. What evidence supports your decision-making?

992. Who should attend?

993. What future plans (e.g., modifications) do you have for your program?

994. What is the large, desired outcome?

995. What are the evaluation strategies (e.g., reaction, learning, behavior, results) used. What evaluation results did you have?

996. Does platform-specific assessment information contribute to training placement or tailoring of instruction (e.g. aptitude-treatment interaction)?

3.10 Issue Log: SAP Business One

997. Are the SAP Business One project issues uniquely identified, including to which product they refer?

998. Is access to the Issue Log controlled?

999. Why do you manage human resources?

1000. Are stakeholder roles recognized by your organization?

1001. Can an impact cause deviation beyond team, stage or SAP Business One project tolerances?

1002. How were past initiatives successful?

1003. Which team member will work with each stakeholder?

1004. What steps can you take for positive relationships?

1005. How do you manage communications?

1006. What is the stakeholders level of authority?

1007. How do you reply to this question; you am new here and managing this major program. How do you suggest you build your network?

1008. Which stakeholders are thought leaders, influences, or early adopters?

1009. What are the typical contents?

1010. Who were proponents/opponents?

1011. Do you prepare stakeholder engagement plans?

1012. Do you often overlook a key stakeholder or stakeholder group?

4.0 Monitoring and Controlling Process Group: SAP Business One

1013. What resources are necessary?

1014. Purpose: toward what end is the evaluation being conducted?

1015. Did the SAP Business One project team have the right skills?

1016. Use: how will they use the information?

1017. Who needs to be involved in the planning?

1018. What will you do to minimize the impact should a risk event occur?

1019. How well did the chosen processes produce the expected results?

1020. How to ensure validity, quality and consistency?

1021. What do they need to know about the SAP Business One project?

1022. How will staff learn how to use the deliverables?

1023. Accuracy: what design will lead to accurate information?

1024. What good practices or successful experiences or transferable examples have been identified?

1025. Is the schedule for the set products being met?

1026. Were escalated issues resolved promptly?

1027. Just how important is your work to the overall success of the SAP Business One project?

1028. Is there adequate validation on required fields?

1029. Did the SAP Business One project team have enough people to execute the SAP Business One project plan?

1030. Did you implement the program as designed?

4.1 Project Performance Report: SAP Business One

1031. What is the degree to which rules govern information exchange between groups?

1032. To what degree are fresh input and perspectives systematically caught and added (for example, through information and analysis, new members, and senior sponsors)?

1033. Next Steps?

1034. To what degree does the information network provide individuals with the information they require?

1035. How is the data used?

1036. To what degree are the members clear on what they are individually responsible for and what they are jointly responsible for?

1037. To what degree are the structures of the formal organization consistent with the behaviors in the informal organization?

1038. To what degree do team members agree with the goals, relative importance, and the ways in which achievement will be measured?

1039. How will procurement be coordinated with other SAP Business One project aspects, such as scheduling and performance reporting?

1040. To what degree are the goals ambitious?

1041. To what degree does the informal organization make use of individual resources and meet individual needs?

1042. How can SAP Business One project sustainability be maintained?

1043. To what degree do team members understand one anothers roles and skills?

1044. To what degree do members articulate the goals beyond the team membership?

1045. To what degree are the tasks requirements reflected in the flow and storage of information?

4.2 Variance Analysis: SAP Business One

1046. How do you evaluate the impact of schedule changes, work around, et?

1047. Is the entire contract planned in time-phased control accounts to the extent practicable?

1048. How does the monthly budget compare to the actual experience?

1049. Are the wbs and organizational levels for application of the SAP Business One projected overhead costs identified?

1050. Are there changes in the overhead pool and/or organization structures?

1051. Are the overhead pools formally and adequately identified?

1052. Does the scheduling system identify in a timely manner the status of work?

1053. Do you identify potential or actual budget-based and time-based schedule variances?

1054. Is the anticipated (firm and potential) business base SAP Business One projected in a rational, consistent manner?

1055. There are detailed schedules which support

control account and work package start and completion dates/events?

1056. Are there knowledgeable SAP Business One projections of future performance?

1057. At what point should variances be isolated and brought to the attention of the management?

1058. Who are responsible for overhead performance control of related costs?

1059. Favorable or unfavorable variance?

1060. Are there externalities from having some customers, even if they are unprofitable in the short run?

1061. What causes selling price variance?

1062. How do you identify and isolate causes of favorable and unfavorable cost and schedule variances?

1063. Are management actions taken to reduce indirect costs when there are significant adverse variances?

1064. Did a new competitor enter the market?

1065. How do you verify authorization to proceed with all authorized work?

4.3 Earned Value Status: SAP Business One

1066. Verification is a process of ensuring that the developed system satisfies the stakeholders agreements and specifications; Are you building the product right? What do you verify?

1067. Validation is a process of ensuring that the developed system will actually achieve the stakeholders desired outcomes; Are you building the right product? What do you validate?

1068. Are you hitting your SAP Business One projects targets?

1069. How does this compare with other SAP Business One projects?

1070. Where is evidence-based earned value in your organization reported?

1071. When is it going to finish?

1072. What is the unit of forecast value?

1073. How much is it going to cost by the finish?

1074. Earned value can be used in almost any SAP Business One project situation and in almost any SAP Business One project environment. it may be used on large SAP Business One projects, medium sized SAP Business One projects, tiny SAP Business One projects (in cut-down form), complex and simple SAP Business One projects and in any market sector. some people, of course, know all about earned value, they have used it for years - but perhaps not as effectively as they could have?

1075. Where are your problem areas?

1076. If earned value management (EVM) is so good in determining the true status of a SAP Business One project and SAP Business One project its completion, why is it that hardly any one uses it in information systems related SAP Business One projects?

4.4 Risk Audit: SAP Business One

1077. Does the adoption of a business risk audit approach change internal control documentation and testing practices?

1078. Does your auditor understand your business?

1079. Extending the consideration on the halo effect, to what extent are auditors able to build skepticism in evidence review?

1080. How will you maximise opportunities?

1081. Do you have a realistic budget and do you present regular financial reports that identify how you are going against that budget?

1082. What events or circumstances could affect the achievement of your objectives?

1083. Tradeoff: how much risk can be tolerated and still deliver the products where they need to be?

1084. Have you considered the health and safety of everyone in your organization and do you meet work health and safety regulations?

1085. What are the outcomes you are looking for?

1086. Have all involved been advised of any obligations they have to sponsors?

1087. Does your organization have any policies or

procedures to guide its decision-making (code of conduct for the board, conflict of interest policy, etc.)?

1088. Do you have proper induction processes for all new paid staff and volunteers who have a specific role and responsibility?

1089. Has risk management been considered when planning an event?

1090. Will safety checks of personal equipment supplied by competitors be conducted?

1091. Is the auditor able to evaluate contradictory evidence in an unbiased manner?

1092. What expertise do auditors need to generate effective business-level risk assessments, and to what extent do auditors currently possess the already stated attributes?

1093. Have staff received necessary training?

1094. Are policies communicated to all affected?

4.5 Contractor Status Report: SAP Business One

1095. What was the final actual cost?

1096. What was the budget or estimated cost for your organizations services?

1097. Are there contractual transfer concerns?

1098. How does the proposed individual meet each requirement?

1099. How long have you been using the services?

1100. What process manages the contracts?

1101. Who can list a SAP Business One project as organization experience, your organization or a previous employee of your organization?

1102. What was the actual budget or estimated cost for your organizations services?

1103. What are the minimum and optimal bandwidth requirements for the proposed soluiton?

1104. What was the overall budget or estimated cost?

1105. If applicable; describe your standard schedule for new software version releases. Are new software version releases included in the standard maintenance plan?

1106. What is the average response time for answering a support call?

1107. Describe how often regular updates are made to the proposed solution. Are corresponding regular updates included in the standard maintenance plan?

1108. How is risk transferred?

4.6 Formal Acceptance: SAP Business One

1109. Does it do what SAP Business One project team said it would?

1110. Do you buy-in installation services?

1111. Who supplies data?

1112. What function(s) does it fill or meet?

1113. Was the sponsor/customer satisfied?

1114. Was the client satisfied with the SAP Business One project results?

1115. Was the SAP Business One project work done on time, within budget, and according to specification?

1116. What lessons were learned about your SAP Business One project management methodology?

1117. What are the requirements against which to test, Who will execute?

1118. Did the SAP Business One project achieve its MOV?

1119. Do you perform formal acceptance or burn-in tests?

1120. Was business value realized?

1121. How does your team plan to obtain formal acceptance on your SAP Business One project?

1122. Do you buy pre-configured systems or build your own configuration?

1123. What can you do better next time?

1124. What features, practices, and processes proved to be strengths or weaknesses?

1125. Have all comments been addressed?

1126. Was the SAP Business One project goal achieved?

1127. Does it do what client said it would?

1128. What was done right?

5.0 Closing Process Group: SAP Business One

1129. Just how important is your work to the overall success of the SAP Business One project?

1130. How will you do it?

1131. How well did the team follow the chosen processes?

1132. What areas were overlooked on this SAP Business One project?

1133. Did you do what you said you were going to do?

1134. What could have been improved?

1135. Specific - is the objective clear in terms of what, how, when, and where the situation will be changed?

1136. What areas does the group agree are the biggest success on the SAP Business One project?

1137. Are there funding or time constraints?

1138. What will you do?

1139. Was the schedule met?

1140. Did the SAP Business One project team have enough people to execute the SAP Business One project plan?

1141. How dependent is the SAP Business One project on other SAP Business One projects or work efforts?

1142. Were cost budgets met?

1143. Contingency planning. if a risk event occurs, what will you do?

1144. What was learned?

5.1 Procurement Audit: SAP Business One

1145. Audits: when was your last independent public accountant (ipa) audit and what were the results?

1146. Is the purchasing department responsible for a continual review of marketing trends, particularly on long-term contracts and contracts containing escalation clauses?

1147. Are advance payments to employees properly authorized and controlled?

1148. Are goods generally ordered and received in time to be used in the programs for which they were ordered?

1149. Were calculations used in evaluation adequate and correct?

1150. Are there procedures to ensure that changes to purchase orders will be updated on the computer files?

1151. Were bids properly evaluated?

1152. Did your organization identify the full contract value and include options and provisions for renewals?

1153. Is the approval graduated according to the amount disbursed?

1154. Is the purchase order form clear and complete so that the vendor understands all terms and conditions?

1155. Are all mutilated and voided checks retained for proper accounting of pre-numbered checks?

1156. Does the strategy ensure that needs are met, and not exceeded?

1157. Where applicable, did your organization adequately manage experts employed to assist in the procurement process?

1158. Are there mechanisms in place to evaluate the performance of the departments suppliers?

1159. Are all complaints of late or incorrect payment sent to a person independent of the already stated having cash disbursement responsibilities?

1160. Are there systems for recording and monitoring in order to discover malpractice and fraud in the procurement function/unit?

1161. Are procurement policies and practices in line with (international) good practice standards?

1162. Do you learn from benchmarking your own practices with international standards?

1163. Are contract changes after awarding properly justified and executed?

1164. Is there no evidence of collusion between

bidders?

5.2 Contract Close-Out: SAP Business One

1165. Change in knowledge?

1166. Have all contracts been completed?

1167. Have all contracts been closed?

1168. Change in circumstances?

1169. Parties: Authorized?

1170. Change in attitude or behavior?

1171. Was the contract complete without requiring numerous changes and revisions?

1172. What happens to the recipient of services?

1173. Was the contract sufficiently clear so as not to result in numerous disputes and misunderstandings?

1174. Are the signers the authorized officials?

1175. How does it work?

1176. What is capture management?

1177. How/when used ?

1178. Have all contract records been included in the SAP Business One project archives?

1179. How is the contracting office notified of the automatic contract close-out?

1180. Has each contract been audited to verify acceptance and delivery?

1181. Parties: who is involved?

1182. Was the contract type appropriate?

1183. Why Outsource?

1184. Have all acceptance criteria been met prior to final payment to contractors?

5.3 Project or Phase Close-Out: SAP Business One

1185. How much influence did the stakeholder have over others?

1186. Who is responsible for award close-out?

1187. What process was planned for managing issues/risks?

1188. What was the preferred delivery mechanism?

1189. What are the marketing communication needs for each stakeholder?

1190. Who controlled the resources for the SAP Business One project?

1191. Is the lesson significant, valid, and applicable?

1192. What are they?

1193. What hierarchical authority does the stakeholder have in your organization?

1194. In preparing the Lessons Learned report, should it reflect a consensus viewpoint, or should the report reflect the different individual viewpoints?

1195. What are the informational communication needs for each stakeholder?

1196. Who exerted influence that has positively affected or negatively impacted the SAP Business One project?

1197. Were messages directly related to the release strategy or phases of the SAP Business One project?

1198. What is a Risk Management Process?

1199. Complete yes or no?

1200. Were risks identified and mitigated?

1201. Which changes might a stakeholder be required to make as a result of the SAP Business One project?

1202. What can you do better next time, and what specific actions can you take to improve?

1203. Does the lesson educate others to improve performance?

5.4 Lessons Learned: SAP Business One

1204. How well were SAP Business One project issues communicated throughout your involvement in the SAP Business One project?

1205. How timely was the training you received in preparation for the use of the product/service?

1206. How efficient were SAP Business One project team meetings conducted?

1207. Is your organization willing to expose problems or mistakes for the betterment of the collective whole, and can you do this in a way that does not intimidate employees or workers?

1208. Who managed most of the communication within the SAP Business One project?

1209. How effectively and timely was your organizational change impact identified and planned for?

1210. What SAP Business One project circumstances were not anticipated?

1211. How well does the product or service the SAP Business One project produced meet the defined SAP Business One project requirements?

1212. Were quality procedures built into the SAP

Business One project?

1213. How effective was the support you received during implementation of the product/service?

1214. If issue escalation was required, how effectively were issues resolved?

1215. How timely were Progress Reports provided to the SAP Business One project Manager by Team Members?

1216. How effectively were issues managed on the SAP Business One project?

1217. How well were expectations met regarding the frequency and content of information that was conveyed to by the SAP Business One project Manager?

1218. How effective was the training you received in preparation for the use of the product/service?

1219. Overall, how effective was the performance of the SAP Business One project Manager?

1220. How complete and timely were the materials you were provided to decide whether to proceed from one SAP Business One project lifecycle phase to the next?

1221. How much flexibility is there in the funding (e.g., what authorities does the program manager have to change to the specifics of the funding within the overall funding ceiling)?

1222. Was the change control process properly implemented to manage changes to cost, scope, schedule, or quality?

1223. What were the main sources of frustration in the SAP Business One project?

Index

repeatable 203
rephrased 11
replace 130
replaced 53
replacing 142
replanning 154
replicated 117, 119
report 5-6, 47, 85, 121, 175, 186, 217, 240, 248, 259
reported 153-154, 176, 186, 244
reporting 80, 82, 154, 185, 198, 220, 240
reports 38, 132, 176, 194, 246, 262
repository 194
represent 63, 182, 214, 222
reproduced 1
reputation 101, 121
request 5, 56, 141, 182, 219, 221-222
requested 1, 70, 219-221
requests 208, 219
require 40, 80, 165, 235, 240
required 20, 28-29, 34, 66-67, 140, 142, 150, 157-158, 164, 169, 197, 201-202, 239, 260, 262
requiring 117, 119, 132, 257
research 125, 170, 201, 235
reserved 1
reserves 189, 208
reside 194
residual 153
resolution 57
resolve 230, 233
resolved 174, 239, 262
resource 3-4, 81-83, 85, 92, 136, 142, 153, 160, 165, 167-168, 170, 193, 207, 217, 230
resources 2, 9, 18, 28, 33, 49, 51, 54, 67, 69, 79-80, 83, 103, 106, 112, 123, 143, 156, 158-160, 164, 173, 175, 177, 180, 182, 190, 208, 213, 228, 230, 236, 238, 241, 259
respect 1
responded 13
response 20, 81, 83, 85-86, 249
responsive 172, 179
result 53, 63, 65, 154, 178-179, 185, 195, 221, 257, 260
resultant 210
resulted 79
resulting 59, 137, 147, 153